CHRIS POLLARD
SIOBHAN McGINN

Cogan & Mater

Contents

Key to symbols

- **⓪** **Place number**
- **☕** **Café**
- **✖** **Restaurant**
- **🛏** **Hotel**
- **🛒** **Shop**
- **⊗** **Closed days**
- **🕐** **Opening times**
- **🍷** **Number of beers**
- **🍴** **Food**

Published by Cogan & Mater Limited.

© Cogan & Mater Limited 2006.
Managing Editor: Tim Webb

All rights reserved. No part of this publication
may be reproduced, stored in any retrieval system,
or transmitted, in any form or by any means,
electronic, mechanical, photocopying,
recording or otherwise, without the prior
permission of the copyright owner.

First Published 2006

Printed in the United Kingdom at the
University Press, Cambridge.

Book design: Dale Tomlinson
Typeface: OT Versa (*by Peter Verheul*)
Maps: John Macklin
All photographs: Pollard & McGinn,
with extra photos supplied by Filip Geerts, Inge,
Jeremy Gray, Phil Platt. A special thank you to
Marc Struyf for his help with beer labels.

ISBN 0 9547789 1 X

Around Bruges in 80 Beers has not accepted
advertising or received any other form of
payment or deal from any of the cafés,
restaurants, hotels, breweries, shops or
boats featured in its pages. All entries
were chosen entirely on their merits.

Welkom!

BRUGES is many people's first experience of Belgium. It attracts some two million visitors every year from all over the world. It is one of Europe's top weekend destinations and is particularly handy for visitors from Britain, being less than an hour from Brussels Eurostar terminal and the Channel ports.

Bruges deserves its reputation as a lovely, unspoilt medieval city, famed for its architecture, lace and chocolates. However, it is also a great place to sample the diverse offerings of Belgium's finest brewers. How many other cities can offer 80 hugely different places selling 80 different top quality beers?

After many years of visiting and drinking in the city we decided it was time to share our knowledge and point people to the cafés, restaurants and shops that stock the best beers. Around Bruges in 80 Beers is aimed at the general traveller who knows that Belgian beer is supposed to be good and wants to know where they can try the best, in the most interesting surroundings.

We have matched each of the 80 places with a specific beer, chosen from their menu. This is not to say that they cannot be found at other cafés in Bruges or indeed throughout Belgium. The places we have chosen range from specialist beer shops to posh restaurants, from locals' bars to elegant taverns and from early risers to late night haunts. We even have a boat.

There is no end to the places where you can drink dull, factory-produced, brand name beers from multi-national producers with huge advertising budgets. We will lead you instead to quality Belgian beers, many unknown outside Belgium and sometimes even outside the area where they are brewed.

We have included beers from old family-run breweries, tiny new micro-breweries and some that will be like nothing you have ever tasted before.

Armed with this guide, you should be able to dig a little deeper and be more adventurous in your beer choices and to experience some of the truly exceptional offerings of the greatest brewing nation in the world. You will find out with practice, which beer styles and which beers you prefer.

And if 80 proves a bit too much for even a long weekend, we may just persuade you to return, again and again.

We hope you enjoy reading, and more importantly, using this book as much as we enjoyed researching it.

CHEERS!

Podge & Siobhan

Listings

Beer shops

- ① Bacchus Cornelius
- ⑦ Bier Paleis
- ⑧ Bier Tempel
- ⑥① Smatch

Hotels and hostels

- ④ Bauhaus
- ②⑧ Ganzespel
- ③③ Passage
- ⑥② Snuffel (BUDGET)
- ①② Boterhuis
- ②⑤ Erasmus
- ⑦⑥ 't Zand (★★★)
- ⑤⑧ Huyze Die Maene
- ④⑨ Meeting – Oud Huis Relais (★★
- ⑤⑦ Pergola – Die Swaene (★★★★★)

Cafés with great beer lists

- ③ Bargehuis (125 different beers)
- ①④ Brugs Beertje (250)
- ①⑤ Cambrinus (400)
- ②② Dickie's (70+)
- ②⑤ Erasmus (125)
- ②⑨ Garre (125)
- ④⓪ Kelk (60+)
- ④④ Kuppe (80+)
- ⑤③ Oude Speye (210)
- ⑦⓪ Tuinbos (150)
- ⑦⑧ Zolder (54)

Restaurants

⑤ **Begintje** (CLASSIC FLEMISH)
⑨ **B-In** (MODERN EXOTIC)
⑩ **Bon Vivant** (GRILLS)
⑪ **Botanieske** (VARIED)
⑫ **Boterhuis** (FLEMISH)
⑰ **Celtic Ireland** (IRISH EUROPEAN)
⑲ **Curiosa** (BISTRO)
⑳ **Damsche Clipper** (FLEMISH)
㉑ **Dell'Arte** (BISTRO)
㉒ **Dickie's** (GRILLS)
㉓ **Dijver** (CLASSIC FLEMISH)
㉕ **Erasmus** (MODERN FLEMISH)
㉘ **Ganzespel** (FLEMISH)
㉜ **Gouden Aap** (BISTRO)
㉝ **Gran Kaffee de Passage** (CLASSIC FLEMISH)
㉞ **Gruuthuse Hof** (CLASSIC FLEMISH)
㊳ **Huyze Die Maene** (FLEMISH)
㊼ **Lokkedize** (GREEK)
㊽ **Lunatic** (BISTRO)
(51) **Nieuw Museum** (GRILLS)
(52) **Nisse** (FISH & FONDUE)
(55) **Pallieterke** (FLEMISH)
(56) **Panier d'Or** (FISH)
(57) **Pergola** (MODERN FLEMISH)
(58) **Pietje Pek** (FLEMISH)
(59) **Republiek** (WORLD)
(60) **Schijverke** (FRENCH/FLEMISH)
(63) **Stoepa** (EASTERN)
(65) **Strijdershuis** (MODERN FLEMISH)
(71) **Uilenspiegel** (FLEMISH/GREEK)
(72) **Verloren Hoek** (FLEMISH)
(73) **Vlaamsche Pot** (CLASSIC FLEMISH)
(76) **'t Zand** (BISTRO)
(77) **Zandloper** (FLEMISH)
(80) **Zwijntje** (PORK)

Family pubs

③ **Bargehuis**
(58) **Pietje Pek** (EATING)
(59) **Republiek**
(79) **Zwarte Kat**

Specials

④ **Bauhaus** (INTERNET)
⑨ **B-In** (ULTRAMODERN)
⑬ **Bretoen Pannenkoeken** (PANCAKE HOUSE)
⑱ **Coffee Link** (INTERNET)
㉗ **Ezeltje** (DONKEY BAR)
㉟ **Halve Maan** (BREWERY)
㊴ **Jerry's** (CIGAR BAR)
㊸ **Kogge** (TINY)
㊺ **Lamme Goedzak** (BOAT)
(66) **Tempelier** (ARCHERY)
(74) **Vlissinghe** (ANCIENT)
(79) **Zwarte Kat** (MUSEUM)

Belgian beer styles – a simple guide

Kriek–
a lambic in which cherries have been steeped for six months to create a sweet and sharp drink in which the cherry taste may be anywhere from subtle to intense. Poor quality krieks use fruit syrup. Where no lambic is used the name should be *kriekenbier*.

Dubbel–
the Flemish Dutch word for double, implying double malt in the brew and so double strength. Usually a brown ale of 6–8%, often with allusions to monks or abbeys and sometimes made to raise money for same.

Lambic–
any of the beer styles made using beer that has been fermented with wild yeast taken from the atmosphere. Traditional lambics are fermented in oak casks for up to three years and used mainly for blending to make *gueuze* (above) or steeping with fruit.

Gueuze– traditional (*oude*) gueuze is made from blending two or more lambics (below) and adding a tiny amount of sugar to spark refermentation while it lies in the cellar in champagne-style bottles. The end effect is a unique taste experience somewhere between finest traditional cider, vintage wine and an ultra-dry ale.

Saison–
originally a well-hopped, light summer beer style from Wallonie, the French-speaking south. Nowadays the term "farmhouse ale" is beginning to encompass all the blonde, ambrée and brune styles of beer from the Wallonian microbreweries.

Tripel – the Flemish Dutch word for triple, implying three times the malt/strength. Historically a dark brown strong ale style but nowadays usually a golden-blond, sweetish beer, again sometimes sanctioned to raise money for abbeys, sometimes not.

Stout – local West Flanders' stouts tend to be low strength (4–5%) and sweet, in the manner of an old British milk stout like Mackeson. Others resemble more the dry, bitter Export Guinness style (8–9%).

White beer – typically a lighter (4–5.5%) beer made with at least 30% wheat in the recipe, which causes a natural hazy ("white") appearance. Most are flavoured with coriander, dried peel and other spices.

Trappist beer – an ale produced at one of the seven officially designated breweries sited within an abbey of the Trappist order of monks, six of which are found in Belgium. The majority are strong brown ales though a few are lighter in colour and or strength.

NOTE: throughout this book the %age figures given for beer strength refer to their alcohol by volume. Typical British or American beers are roughly 3.5–4.5%, European lagers 5% and table wines 11–12.5%

Flemish café cuisine

There is a lot more to Flemish cooking than mussels and chips. Culinary excellence is a national obsession and its quality and diversity always impresses visitors. Most of the city's restaurants will describe their more elaborate dishes on English menus. Here are just a few of the commonly encountered bar meals.

Americaine – *cannibaal* (below) with a raw egg yolk.

Asperges – Belgian asparagus, most revered when it is white, monstrous and plumped up. The traditional Flemish way of serving is with chopped egg in melted butter.

Brochette – a proper kebab, featuring steak pieces skewered and char-grilled, typically with slices of onion and peppers.

Cannibaal – raw fillet of beef ground in mayonnaise with a little paprika, usually served on toast with raw carrot, gherkins, silverskin onions and Worcestershire sauce.

Carbonnade – beef, slowed cooked with a few vegetables in sour brown ale, with a little cream added.

Frites – the famous Belgian chips, lightly parboiled then twice fried. Belgians have stopped adding mayonnaise since the tourists started to do so.

Kip (*aan 't spit*) – chicken, impaled on a spit and roasted in front of the flame.

Kikkerbillen – frogs' legs, usually of the small variety, acting mainly as an excuse for garlic and other sauces.

Mosselen – mussels, typically brought to the boil in a cooking pot with beer, celery, onion and herbs and served by the pot-load with *frites*.

Pannekoeken – pancakes (Fr. *crêpes*), usually offered with a variety of sweet or savoury fillings.

Paling in 't groen – eel, cooked in a sauce of green herbs, typically chervil.

Stoemp – mashed potato with carrot, leek or other vegetables in it, originally a Brussels speciality.

Stoofvlees – traditionally made from horse meat but nowadays usually beef, a thick meat and gravy stew that is slow-cooked for hours, sometimes in beer.

Uitsmijter – sliced cold ham on bread topped with three fried eggs, often served with mayonnaise and salad.

Vispannetje – mixed fish pieces in a creamy, sometimes cheesy sauce, cooked on a griddle in a cast iron pan.

Wafel – the Belgian waffle (Fr. *gauffre*).

Waterzooi – the traditional Ghent version of this creamy vegetable stew includes a whole chicken. Chicken pieces are more usual now. Coastal West Flanders has a fish version.

Witloof – white chicory, often served wrapped in ham and baked in a cheese sauce. The vegetable was first grown commercially in Belgium.

The various types of steak – *entrecôte, pave, Châteaubriand, filet* and others are presented with sauces such as *Bearnaise* (tarragon butter sauce), *archiduc* (mushroom), *Provençale* (Mediterranean vegetable), *Roquefort* (blue cheese) or *au poivre* (green peppercorn cream).

DUTCH–ENGLISH MENU TRANSLATOR

eend	duck
everzwijn	wild boar
forel	trout
garnalen	shrimps
haas	hare
haring	herring
heilbot	halibut
kabeljauw	cod
konijn	rabbit
lamsvlees	lamb
Ostendaise	in a shrimp sauce
parelhoen	guinea fowl
patrijs	partridge
roomsaus	in a cream sauce
schol	plaice
staartvis	monkfish
tarbot	turbot
varken	pork
Vlaamse	Flemish
witloof	chicory
zalm	salmon
zeeduivel	monkfish
zeetong	Dover sole
zeewolf	sea bass

Bacchus Cornelius

1 Bacchus Cornelius 🛒
17 Academiestraat
T 050 34 53 38
F 050 351 91 83
E info@bacchuscornelius.com
www.bacchuscornelius.com
⊗ Sunday (Jan–Nov); & Wednesday
🕐 10.00–18.30
🍸 400+
🍽 None

Beer shop with a huge range from all over the country including some sold nowhere else in the city.

You will often find tourists nearby with their cameras pointing upwards towards the small statue of the Bruges Bear, set in the Poortersloge building opposite. He is frequently dressed in weird and wonderful clothes, in the tradition of Brussels' Mannekin Pis.

The featured beer here is Pannepot from De Struise Brouwers. The name comes from the type of boat that worked the coast at De Panne near the French border. The one pictured on the label is the P-50 owned by an ancestor of one of the brewers.

De Struise Brouwers are a group of friends who started to home-brew beer at their ostrich farm in Lo, a small town out towards the battlefields. When it proved popular they asked Caulier brewery of Péruwelz near Tournai to brew it for them commercially and recently moved the production contract to Deca of Woesten in West Flanders.

Pannepot (10%) has a warm deep brown colour and a dense, creamy head. It is strongly aromatic with lots of fruit, coffee and chocolate aromas. The taste is powerful but well-balanced with a rich, stout-like character that is inwardly warming. It packs a mighty punch and should be savoured slowly.

14

2 BaraBass 🍷
43 Sint Clarastraat
T 050 34 50 34
⊗ Monday (school holidays); & Sunday
🍺 Friday 11.00–01.00;
Saturday to 03.00;
Monday to 23.00;
others to 21.00
🍷 23
🍴 Small snacks, including *croques*

Set in the north of the city fifteen minutes walk from the old centre, BaraBass is the second oldest licensed premise in Bruges, after Vlissinghe (below). It first became a café in 1712 and its frontage is protected, recognising its former role as a Guild House.

This is a temple to the old British brewery, Bass, using a huge quantity of memorabilia from that company as decoration. There is even a triangular bar in the shape of the Bass logo. Its large single room is homely and there is a garden terrace at the rear. There is a fine old stone fireplace, of typical Brugean design, man and wife pillars at each end, wearing medieval headgear.

Despite its antiquity, this café lives in the present, with a youthful evening crowd. Bass was world-famous for two centuries before being consigned to "brand heaven" in the global takeover war. The modern bottled version is available but should be drunk in remembrance of times past.

Our featured beer here is the increasingly world-famous **Westmalle Tripel** (9.5%) brewed at a Trappist abbey in the north of the country. This beer is available in many Belgian cafés and is often a godsend, appropriately.

It is amber-blond in colour with a powerful, smooth taste that can be enjoyed in the day but is more suited to late evening drinking. This is the *tripel* that all others are judged against. Its strength determines it should be revered, so careful now!

Bargehuis

3 Bargehuis
2 Bargeweg
T 050 33 26 04
F 050 34 26 40
E info@bargehuis.be
www.bargehuis.be
⊗ Monday
From 11.00
125
Bar meals including spit-roasted chicken and ribs, plus a good vegetarian selection.

The "Barge House" can be found at the end of Katelijnestraat just before you hit Katelijnepoort on the ring road, not far from the station.

It aims at a wide audience and is particularly appealing for family parties. There are lots of toys inside for kiddies and an outside garden play area and sandpit at the front. There is even a separate children's menu.

The building has a number of rooms, some of which are huge and cater for large drinking and eating groups. Toilets have disabled access.

Try to make your visit coincide with the annual Beer Festival in August where beer is given away ... we kid you not.

It is a great place for beer drinkers the rest of the year too with a beer menu of 125 choices, some rarely seen in Bruges. Beers on offer include several Moinette brews from Dupont, Bon Secours from Caulier, Achouffe beers and a wide range from De Dolle Brouwers.

The beer recommended here is **Pater Lieven Blond** (6.5%) from Van den Bossche brewery, a small family-owned firm south of Ghent. It is a golden pale ale with a light but balanced taste.

Anno 1897

Pater Lieven
Blond - Blonde
Abdijbier - Bière d'abbaye
Belgisch Bier - Bière Belge

Bauhaus 🍺 ✕ 🛏

133–137 Langestraat

T 050 34 10 93
F 050 33 41 80
E info@bauhaus.be
www.bauhaus.be/restaurants.html
Open all week

🕐 08.00–02.00

🍷 27

🍴 Bar meals, including pasta & pizzas, chilli, chicken Creole and steaks.

The Bauhaus is best known as a budget hotel but also has a café-restaurant with two very different rooms.

The first is basic, laid back and aimed at young backpackers. The second is a bit of a surprise. It has an eastern *seraglio* feel with a dimly lit black slate runway down the middle, bronze inlaid tables, a huge clock on the wall and leopard print seats. Eclectic or what!

There is also an internet café for those missing home and its computer comforts.

Food (12.00–14.00; 18.00–23.00, 24.00 weekends) is good value.

On the beery side, the bar stocks the famous mighty **Bush Ambrée** (12%) from the Dubuisson family brewery, between Tournai and Mons. This is a huge, hearty barley wine, one of the strongest beers in Belgium. It is an amber coloured, sweet sipping beer that warms all the way down – a perfect nightcap.

Begijntje

5 Begijntje
11 Walstraat
T 050 33 00 89
F 050 33 00 89
E info@restaurantbegijntje.be
www.restaurantbegijntje.be
⊗ Tuesday & Wednesday
🕐 From 12.00
🍷 19
Full restaurant menu includes
fish dishes, steaks and ostrich!

The Begijntje may be one of Bruges'
smallest restaurants but it has a big reputation. Newspaper cuttings on the walls
trumpet the food quality, its fish soup
being picked out for particular praise.

It has a drinking terrace outside in
season onto Walplein square, opposite
the Halve Maan brewery, where you will
get a good view of the passing horse-
drawn carriages – this is tourist Bruges!

Inside the tiny restaurant has Flemish
tapestry wallpaper, hanging copper pots,

and a treacherous spiral staircase
leading to the first floor toilets.

The beer menu features beers from
the family-owned Bavik brewery, near
Kortrijk. Their **Pilaarbijter Blond**
(7.2%) is a relative newcomer to
the scene and is a beer of quality.
It is a golden blond, spicy brew.

The beer label is unusual and
features a man biting a pillar,
taken from Pieter Breugel's famous
painting "The Flemish Proverbs."
In Dutch a 'Pillar Biter' is a hypocrite.

6 De Belleman Pub
22 Jozef Suveestraat
T 050 34 19 89
✗ Sunday & Monday
🕐 11.00–01.00
🍷 28
🍴 Light snacks, including pasta, omelettes and smoked salmon.

The tradition of the Belleman or "town crier" has existed in Belgium as long as it has in England and the country has hosted the annual world championship of such things.

This street-corner bar is to be found on the way from Vismarkt to Astrid Park, one of inner Bruges' better kept secrets – a tranquil park and duck pond that can be spared the crowds even in summer.

This English-pub-style bar has raised red velvet banquette seating and an aura of cosiness. They have collections of steins and banknotes and enough newspapers to keep abreast of world events, as long as your Dutch is good enough.

Here you can try Oeral from De Dolle Brouwers, rebadged as Museum Beer.

De Dolle Brouwers were at the vanguard of the renaissance of Belgian beer at the start of the 1980's. They remain at the forefront of Belgian brewing for quality and innovation. The brewery, which is about 20 kilometres away near Diksmuide, can be visited on Sunday afternoons.

Oeral (6%) is a straw-coloured beer with a fresh, hoppy, dry taste.

MUSEUM BIER
Hooistraat 42
8000 Brugge
Tel. 050/33 12 96
Fax. 050/33 12 22

33cl

DE DOLLE BROUWERS W••••

Bierpaleis

7 Bierpaleis
25–27 Katelijnestraat
T 050 34 31 61
F 050 34 05 10
E info@bierpaleis.com
Open all week
🕐 10.00–19.00
🍷 250+
None

The Beer Palace is one of the city's top beer shops, especially if you are on the lookout for rare beer glasses.

They probably have the largest range of glassware anywhere in town and you can buy the beers to go with them. There are also serious quantities of souvenirs, gifts, football shirts and scarves.

The shop sells all of the well-known quality Belgian beers and some rarities too. They also commission a beer from the Proef brewery at Lochristi, between Ghent and Antwerp, who make beers to their customers' own recipes. The result in this case is Babbelaer, a favourite beer here among the many.

If you want to buy lots of beers, but do not want to carry them home, then the shop offers worldwide shipping.

Our featured beer is a rarity from Wallonia, the unique **Fantôme** (8%). This is a hazy, golden ale with a dry, fruity, citrus flavour. This beer in the *saison* style comes in 75cl corked bottle and is brewed by Dany Prignon's Fantôme Brewery at Soy, deep in the Ardennes, in Luxembourg province.

8 Bier Tempel

7 Philipstockstraat
- **T** 050 34 37 30
- **F** 050 34 37 30
- Open all week
- 10.00–19.00
- 400+
- None

The Beer Temple can be found just off Markt.

This attractive beer shop probably has the broadest range of Belgian beers under one roof in Bruges. It is also a good place for beer-based books, maps, gifts and paraphernalia.

The friendly staff are happy to offer expert advice about all aspects of Belgian brewing and know their stuff. If you happen to visit Brussels, the owners run a sister shop in the Marché aux Herbes, near Grand'Place. It has the same name.

This is a great shop in which to buy *gueuze* and *kriek* beers, the selection being second to none in West Flanders. These so-called lambic beers are spontaneously fermented by wild yeast found in the atmosphere. The method is unique to Belgium, with most being brewed in a small area just west of Brussels.

Girardin 'Oude' Gueuze 1882 (5%) is a prime example of the lambic brewer's craft. The word 'Oude' on a label signifies its authenticity as a beer blended only from authentic lambic beers of different ages, some of which are aged for up to three years in their oak casks. The blending results in a pale golden beer, with the sharp, dry, sparkling taste explosion that is the mark of fine *gueuze*.

B-In

9 B-In
Oud Sint Jan complex
Zonnekemeers
T 050 31 13 00
F 050 31 13 00
E info@b-in.be
www.b-in.be
⊗ Tuesday
🕐 11.00–01.00; Fr & Sa to 03.00
🍷 15
🍴 Full restaurant menu, from tapas to exotic
European and Asian specialities

Just in case you thought that Bruges' café society consisted entirely of ancient Flemish interiors with lace curtains and shelves cluttered with waffle irons, we thought we should lead you to B-In.

Although housed in the historic Oud Sint-Jan hospital complex this is a brilliant example of a café that achieves excellence through modern minimalist design, colour and exceptional use of light. Each of its three distinct spaces – restaurant, bar and lounge – has its own character. Bruges' flirtation with modernity does not always harmonise well with the old city but this one works.

You can just drop in for a beer with a view or enjoy the city's most adventurous menu, conjured up by chefs who graduated from Belgium's top schools for the culinary arts.

The beer we suggest you try here is **Liefmans Kriekbier** (6%). This is not a cherry lambic but rather is produced by steeping cherries in aged brown ale. Although slightly sweetened, it is not overly so, its somewhat tart taste leading many Belgians to see it as their country's finest fruit beer.

Le Bon Vivant ✕
10 Dweersstraat
T 050 34 13 27
E lebistrobonvivant@hotmail.com
www.lebistrobonvivant.be
✕ Sunday & Monday
🕐 16.00–02.00
🍺 10
🍴 Full restaurant menu, featuring charcoal grills from scampi and Dover sole to giant skewers of meat.

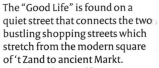

The "Good Life" is found on a quiet street that connects the two bustling shopping streets which stretch from the modern square of 't Zand to ancient Markt.

It describes itself as a nocturnal bistro and devotes itself mainly to food, specialising in serving dishes cooked on a charcoal grill.

Local favourites include pork fillet or ham knuckle, each made with different sauces based on Tongerlo beers.

Drinking without eating is allowed but with such a nice looking menu, you might change your mind and stay a while.

The beer menu is dominated by beers from Belgium's largest independent brewery, Haacht, from near the town of that name in Flemish Brabant. One of the best is **Adler** (6%), a Dortmunder-style lager beer. It is golden-yellow in colour with a solid, white head and a grainy taste like a Pilsener with added malt.

Botaniekske

⑪ 't Botaniekske 🍷 ✖
26 Minderbroedersstraat
T 050 33 27 90 / 0475 89 70 60
E info@botaniekske.be
www.botaniekske.be
✖ Monday & Tuesday
🕐 From 18.00; + Su 12.30–14.30
🍷 20
🍴 Full restaurant menu, including grilled
meat, fish dishes, ribs and braised ham.

The Little Botanical is a nice, small café housed in a building that dates from 1612, with a traditional Flemish interior that includes a pretty stove.

You will find it on one of the corners of Astrid Park at its out-of-town end. The inscription above the stone tiled fireplace reads "Vrienden zien hier thuus" – friends are at home here.

Mood music accompanies your meal. The house specialities are braised ham and spare ribs. The menu is available in Braille. There are special items for children.

The café stocks four beers from the St Bernardus brewery in the hop fields of West Flanders – **Pater 6**, **Tripel**, **Prior 8** and **Abt 12**.

The **Prior 8** (8%) is a dark chestnut dubbel style beer, a little on the sweet side with a hint of pear drops. A fine accompaniment to any of the pork dishes.

⑫ Hotel Boterhuis 🍷 ✕ ⇄

38 St Jakobsstraat

T 050 34 15 11

F 050 34 70 89

E boterhuis@pandora.be

www.hotels-belgium.com/brugge/
boterhuis.htm

Open all week

🕐 10.00–01.00

🍷 32

🍴 Full restaurant menu, including *stoofvlees*, steaks and brochettes.

The Butter House is a three star hotel a couple of minutes walk off the Markt.

Although this is more of a restaurant than a café, you can have a beer without eating if you wish in its long, modern bar.

The food menu is excellent and offers many of the old Flemish regulars including *stoofvlees*, nowadays usually a beef stew though traditionally made from horse meat. There are daily specials too.

A great beer to try at the Boterhuis is **Liefmans Frambozenbier** (5%), a brew for people who say they don't like beer.

Liefmans have been making slightly soured brown ales at Oudenaarde in East Flanders since the 17th century. For know the brewery is used only for fermentation though there are rumours of plans to reinstate brewing too.

Their raspberry beer is presented in a 37.5cl corked, paper-wrapped bottle. It may be a fruit beer but it is not sickly sweet, rather it is a successful combination of both the brown beer base from which it is made and a huge, but not overpowering raspberry flavour.

Bretoen Pannenkoeken

13 Bretoen Pannenkoeken
4 Ezelstraat
T 050 34 23 34
F 050 67 36 58
⊗ Tuesday
🍷 11.30–20.00
🏆 18
🍴 Wide range of sweet and savoury pancakes

This lovely one-roomed café is in the homely style of a Breton kitchen, complete with red checked tablecloths.

This is a *crêperie* or pancake house, where they make 60 sorts of pancakes, prepared, cooked and flambéed before your eyes on the large carousel griddle that dominates the café.

The list of savoury pancakes includes ones stuffed with artichokes or coquilles St Jacques. The Popeye pancake has spinach in a mornay sauce (tasty and huge). Sweet *crêpes* include those flamed with Grand Marnier or Cointreau.

Those who are all beered out can try the gorgeous Normandy cider. This comes in sweet or dry and is served in a stoneware cup or a half litre pitcher.

Beer drinkers are not forgotten though. Try the **Oerbier** (7.5%), the first ever beer from De Dolle Brouwers. This reddish-brown beer is brewed from a recipe that uses six different malts. It has a sharp, tart and distinctive taste. The strapline "Nat en Straf" on the glasses means "wet and strong", a warning of its hidden potency.

14 **'t Brugs Beertje**
5 Kemelstraat

T 050 33 96 16
F 050 33 96 16
E info@brugsbeertje.be
www.brugsbeertje.be
⊗ Wednesday & sometimes Tuesdays
🕐 16.00–01.00
🍺 250
🍴 Light snacks, including pasta

Well where do you start?

The Little Bruges Bear is just off Steenstraat, one of the main shopping streets of Bruges. Since opening in 1982 it has gained worldwide fame. Internationally it has become a beer lovers' shrine and on any night of the year you might find it packed with drinkers of all nations.

So why does this fairly ordinary looking brown bar make it onto the itinerary of beer lover's Grand Tour of Europe? Well, it has a special atmosphere all of its own and although many bars have tried to copy the ambience, none manages to match it. This is a particularly good bar if you are out on your own. Perch on a bar stool and you can as soon find yourself talking to a local as to someone from

Copenhagen, Vermont or Grimsby. Beer is the universal language.

The selection of unusual draught beers changes with the seasons. Owner Daisy Claeys and her staff are supremely knowledgeable about the Belgian beer world and expert at helping out bewildered patrons. The huge beer menu is arranged by region and by brewery.

It is difficult to pick one beer to represent this bar, but we have chosen **Saison Dupont** (6.5%), because it, like the bar, is a world class performer. The first thing you notice on uncorking this golden ale is its distinct flowery aroma. Next comes a billowing hop presence that dominates throughout without bringing unbearable bitterness. It is the most accomplished of the modern versions of a *saison* style beer from Wallonia.

The Dupont brewery is housed in an ancient farm in the village of Tourpes, between Tournai and Mons, in Hainaut province. All *saison* beers were originally brewed on farms, to be drunk by farm workers in the summer months when brewing was impossible due to high temperatures. You can drink this one any time.

Cambrinus

15 Bierbrasserie Cambrinus
19 Philipstockstraat
T 050 33 23 28
w www.cambrinus.eu
Open all week
From 11.00
400
Bar meals, including some cooking with beer

Although the building in which it is housed dates from 1699, the latest incarnation of this café-restaurant, just off Markt, only opened in March 2006.

The name is a corruption of Jan Primus (John the First), one of the early Dukes of Brabant, whose appreciation of the finer things in life extended to excellent ale and banqueting.

The design is English pub style, with dark panelled walls and brass lights. It was created by the same people who converted Dickie's (below) and the legendary Botteltje café in Ostend, though these did not include the hand-painted wall decorations around the bar.

Although you can dine heartily here, they serve everything from nibbles to bar snacks as well. And there is a children's menu.

The beer list is in three languages and tries openly to tempt Pils drinkers into sampling something less boring. Its menu of 400 beers is as daunting as it is brave.

Unusually for Bruges it includes quite a few 75cl bottles, popular for sharing a beer with two or three friends. Among these is **La Rulles Triple** (8.3%), an unspiced strong blonde ale that is full of honeyed and citrus flavours, from the Rulles brewery at Rulles. Perhaps the best of many excellent new breweries in Luxembourg province.

16 't Capucientje
72 Westmeers
T 050 33 92 04
F 050 38 79 81
E info@capucientje.be
www.capucientje.be
⊗ Wednesday (Nov–Mar); Monday
🍷 Tu&Su 11.00–20.00; Th to 18.00;
others to 22.00
🍺 39
🍴 Bar meals, including frogs' legs,
omelettes and scampi.

Capucines can be monks or monkeys. On one of the roads from the railway station to 't Zand, the Little Capucine is one of Flanders' many "tea-rooms". In Belgium that does not just mean that tea is served but also ice cream, pancakes, waffles and apple pie.

Its intelligently picked beer list and wine-of-the-month draws drinkers too.

The café has magazines and on its menus you will find quizzes. From March to November they open their terrace.

Don't tell the children but they do not sell *frites*. See if you can persuade them to try the *kikkerbillen* instead – that means frogs' legs.

Be warned that the owner will offer to take your photo and e-mail it to your home. We took up this kind offer. Sure enough when we got back from our trip we received our photographic souvenir. Sadly the couple enjoying a beer were not us, but a friendly-looking elderly couple we might have liked to meet but never had.

The café stocks the rarely found Reinaert range of beers from Proef brewery including the exceptional **Reinaert Tripel** (9%), one of the few *tripel* beers brewed from an all-malt recipe. This is a hazy, orange-coloured ale with a big, fruity taste that deserves more widespread availability.

Celtic Ireland

17 Celtic Ireland 🍺 ✕

8 Burg
T 050 34 45 02
F 050 34 98 89
E brugge@celticireland.be
www.celticirelandbruges.be
Open all week
🕐 From 11.00
🍷 21
🍴 Bar meals, including lamb stew and Irish haddock

Belgium likes its Irish bars, but does not usually plonk them in the middle of its most historic squares.

The menu states that the interior design is based on the Book of Kells, presumably in its Flemish edition. This bar is all dark red walls, Celtic knots and megaliths. According to the blurb "the beautifully carved wooden bar back will leave a lasting memory" and it does.

There is live music every night, which is quite a feat and there is a TV for the big sporting events.

Surprisingly for an Oirish Bar they do great food. As well as the Hibernian staples – though does a fish really have a nationality – there is a Celtic sandwich featuring, less expectedly perhaps, Cajun chicken on foccacia bread. The spiced monkfish tail is cooked in coconut.

You can find the usual beers such as Guinness and Kilkenny on draught, but for an unusual Belgian, go for **Bourgogne des Flandres** (5.5%), literally Flemish Burgundy, from Timmermans brewery, near Brussels. This dark red beer imitates the Flemish old brown style using a lambic base, tasting sweet, sour and hugely fruity. Slainte!

18 The Coffee Link ⊕
  38 Mariastraat
T 050 34 99 73
E info@thecoffeelink.com
  www.thecoffeelink.com
⊗ Wednesday
🕐 11.00–18.00
🍸 10
🍴 Bar meals including pasta,
  vispannetje and *waterzooi*.

This bright, modern and spacious internet café is part of the Oud Sint-Jan Hospital complex, which was until 1978 one of the oldest hospitals still functioning in Europe.

Nowadays it houses the Hans Memling museum and art gallery, plus a hospital and pharmacy museum.

Coffee was Europe's favourite new psychostimulant drug in the 17th century and 50 varieties are now sold over the counter here, along with 20 types of tea. There is also handy access to worldwide web – not something you get in many modern hospital waiting rooms.

They have a small beer menu, which includes **Brugse Zot Dubbel** (7.5%), a big sister to the blond beer from the city's Halve Maan brewery, just across the canal. It has a rich ruby brown colour and there are smooth sweet roast malt flavours that make it an appealing choice.

Curiosa

19 Taverne Curiosa
22 Vlamingstraat
T 050 34 23 34
F 050 34 23 24
E info@curiosa-brugge.com
www.curiosa-brugge.com
⊗ Monday
🍺 Sa 11.30–01.00; Su to 22.00; others to 23.30
🍷 50
🍴 Full restaurant menu, with salads, grills
including a *Châteaubriand* for two, frogs' l
scampi, fish soup and a great *vispannetje*.

Vlamingstraat runs off the Markt.
Look out for the street sign for this
16th century cellar-bar, which is entered
down some very steep entrance stairs.

Its two rooms have beautiful vaulted
ceilings. Religious icons make for
interesting décor. If you are lucky you
might get the seat next to an odd figure
of Joseph holding
the baby Jesus, whose face has,
rather disconcertingly, fallen off.

Although steak and *frites* is the
obvious favourite here there is a
more adventurous restaurant menu.
Some tables are marked 'No Smoking'.
In Belgium this is more often taken as
an aspiration rather than an instruction.
But it's a start!

Verhaeghe brewery at Vichte near
Kortrijk is one of West Flanders' unsung
heroes. The fourth generation of
Verhaeghes continue to brew and age the
traditional versions of Flemish brown
ale, which is kept in oak tuns for up to
two years before bottling.

Their flagship beer is the deep reddish
brown **Duchesse de Bourgogne** (6.2%)
and this can be found at the Curiosa.
The lovely oaky taste, slightly sour but
deliciously mature may shock initially
but usually wins people over.

Flemish Art of Brewing

DUCHESSE DE BOURGOGNE
Br. Verhaeghe Vichte.

Gasthof de Damsche Clipper 🍷 ⊗
30 Kerkstraat (Damme)
050 67 67 67
Tuesday & Wednesday (*except school holidays*)
From 08.00
30
Full restaurant menu, including
traditionally cooked Polder rabbit
and locally caught fresh Damme eel

An easy half-day trip from Bruges in the old inland port of Damme. This welcome new addition to the drinking spots of Damme takes its name from a type of boat formerly seen on the river Zwin in the days before it silted up, and more recently on the Napoleon canal that runs from Bruges through Damme across into the Netherlands.

There is interesting artwork, often on a theme of river and canal boats, displayed on its wall. This is often for sale, the price list appearing on the menu.

The food here (to 22.00) is traditional too, coming accompanied by suggested beers, all from Bavik brewery at Bavikhove near Kortrijk.

Although we could equally have suggested you try Petrus Oud Bruin or the excellent Aged Pale – a beer aged for eighteen months in oak but made primarily for US beer importers – our chosen beer here is **Bavik Ezel Wit** (5.8%) a darker, grainier and spicier than average wheat beer.

Dell'Arte

28 Vlamingstraat
T 050 34 20 64
F 050 34 20 64
E info@dell-arte.be
www.dell-arte.be
⊗ Thursday & Friday
🕐 Su 11.00–22.00; others from 09.30
🍷 18
🍴 Full restaurant menu, including
filet mignon, traditional lamb stew
and a good selection of fish.

The café Dell'Arte is a colourful tea-room with a Fifties/Sixties retro theme. Despite having a room full of a scary amount of Elvis memorabilia, it maintains a comfortable feel, assisted by old film posters.

Service is fast and attentive. Mechanical features in the toilet do everything except the paperwork.

Food starts with breakfasts, progresses to great lunches, to pancakes and waffles in mid-afternoon and then on to dinner. The menu changes with the seasons.

Although the beer menu is short, it manages to be unusual for Bruges, with for example two Danish beers on draught – **Ceres' Danish Royal Blond** and its excellent **Imperial Stout** (7.7%).

The suggested beer is **Brigand**, from the Van Honsebrouck brewery at Ingelmunster, near Kortrijk. This comes served with a dish of fresh radishes. **Brigand** (9%) is a solid amber beer that drinks its weight and can be so more-ish that it begs a second.

Dickie's

Dickie's Grillhouse
16 Vrijdagmarkt
050 33 59 60
dickiesbeerandgrill@hotmail.com
http://drink.to/dickies
Wednesday
Su from 16.00 (Nov–Mar);
Sa from 09.30; others from 10.30
70+
Full restaurant menu, including
Côte à l'Os and king prawns in garlic

How many bars do you know named after the pub dog? Dickie is the pub's dachshund – the one found shuffling round the bar as if he owns the place.

His beer and grill house can be found on that corner of 't Zand that leads to Smedenpoort, next to the place where coaches from all over Europe drop and pick up their day-trippers. If you are one, make this your first and/or last stop.

During the week grills tend to be an evening thing (to 22.00) though they run all day at the weekend to 23.00). Weekday daytime is lighter snacks, apple pie and home-made ice-cream.

There are usually a couple of special beers on draught, plus a clever list of bottled beers that grows around Christmas time. These tend to come from Belgium's better breweries such as Kerkom near St Truiden in Limburg, Drie Fonteinen of Payottenland, and an exceptional newcomer, Alvinne from Ingelmunster near Kortrijk.

Although many styles of beer are found in Belgium, strong stout is a rarity. One beer maker produces a corker, though. The Ellezelloise brewery is based on an old farm overlooking Ellezelles in northern Hainaut, the place that Agatha Christie saddoes will know was the birthplace of Hercule Poirot.

Hercule (8.4%) is Belgium's premier stout, with a gorgeous burnt coffee chocolate and licquorice flavour and a stoppered bottle.

Dijver

23 Den Dijver ✕
5 Dijver
T 050 33 60 69
F 050 34 10 64
Open all week
🕐 We&Th 12.00–14.00
others 12.00–14.00 & 18.30–21.00
🍷 1 on tap, plus others to match food.
🍴 Full restaurant menu, including
cooking with beer

Named after the canal it borders, the Dijver is one of the restaurants that has led the movement towards fine Belgian beer cuisine.

The dining experience is in the grand style, and the setting and service reflect this. The food is high quality though do not expect massive portions. The menu will always feature something interesting enough to tempt the most jaded palate. Imaginative use is made of fresh local seasonal produce.

To the frustration of some and the relief of many, there is no beer menu to choose from. Rather, each dish is cooked with a specific beer, and you tend to be served with this beer to drink with it. This invariably comes with information about the beer, who brews it and why it is used in the dish you have chosen.

Dining at Den Dyver is a wonderful combination of food and beer, tastes and flavours, though it is wise to make a reservation, as its quality has made it very popular indeed.

You can start your gastronomic experience with a glass of the house beer which is a slightly aged version of **Augustijn** (8%), a blond beer from Van Steenberge brewery of Ertvelde, north of Ghent.

Dolle Dries

Dolle Dries
13 Westmeers
T 050 33 49 15
E info@dolledries.be
www.dolledries.be
Open all week
From 11.00
33
Bar snacks, including sate, Vietnamese spring rolls, sandwiches and salads.

Off another corner of 't Zand sits the Crazy Days café, a two-roomed Flemish-style bar with a tiled floor, chandelier and candlelight.

It lies in the shadow of the imposing new concert hall, a building that had locals up in arms when it opened. It is slowly growing on them, perhaps because its striking vermilion façade is becoming less luminescent with age.

Dolle Dries bills itself as a beer and wine café although they are also big on spirits and cocktails. The good news for the beer drinker is that they do have a few extra beers, outside the norm for the cafés round 't Zand.

Chimay is one of the better known of Belgium's Trappist beers, brewed within the abbey at Scourmont in southern Hainaut, under the auspices of real monks. You will find their beers on many menus throughout the city.

The best is usually the powerful, **Chimay Bleue** (9%). It has the appearance of a big, strong, tough, brown beer but is much simpler on delivery, with hints of roast malt and caramel.

Erasmus

25 **Erasmus** 🍷 ✕ 🛏
35 Wollestraat
T 050 33 57 81
F 050 33 47 27
E info@hotelerasmus.com
www.hotelerasmus.com
✕ Thursday
🕐 12.00–23.00
🍷 125
🍴 Full restaurant menu, including
a wide variety of classic and
new-style Flemish cuisine.

A visit here is compulsory. The owner of the Erasmus, Tom Allewaerts, has been enthusiastic about Belgian beer for over 30 years, in which time he has taken this café, restaurant and hotel through many phases to being a much-loved place for beer enthusiasts from around the world.

The beauty of this place is that you can pop in for a beer and watch the horse carriages go by, you can move through to the restaurant area and choose something sumptuous from the imaginative menu or you can go the whole hog and stay in the ancient-and-modern rooms upstairs.

The café is stylish and peaceful, with classical music, great beer, great food and no sense of rush.

Its beer selection is hard to beat, especially for its breadth of draught beers, which varies on a seasonal basis – Easter beers at Easter, Christmas beers at Christmas etc – and not just from local breweries.

Amongst his finest beers is **XX Bitter** (6.2%) from the De Ranke brewery at Dottignies near Mouscon in northwestern Hainaut, renowned for its massive hop presence. Unlike some of the super-hopped herbal medicines found at modern Californian breweries the dominant flavours here are citric and floral hoppiness, and deploying a top quality malt recipe adds good balance, making this a classic beer.

Estaminet
5 Park
050 33 09 16
Monday
Th from 16.00; others from 11.30
32
Croques and sandwiches only.

Every town has its dependable late night boozers, and often the best of these will have a jazz and blues theme.

There is no British translation of an Estaminet, though Establishment comes close. This one abuts Astrid Park.

It comes to life in the evening, when the jazz and blues soundtrack mixes with the animated conversation of locals. Can it afford to be anything other than dimly lit, with bags of charm. It is an ideal place to drink into the early hours.

In the summer there is a terrace at the front where you can soak up the sun although it is heated for cooler evenings.

The stand out beer on the menu is **Gouden Carolus Classic** (8.5%) from the recently revitalised Anker brewery in Mechelen, south of Antwerp. This big, beefy, dark brown ale has the warm, soothing qualities of an old classic, nowadays once again nudging towards greatness.

Ezeltje

27 't Ezeltje
118 Ezelstraat
T 050 33 25 74
⊗ Tuesday
🕐 Sa&Su 19.00–02.00;
others 12.00–02.00
🍷 24
🍲 Only soup

One of the things that Belgophiles come to love about Belgium is the utterly incongruous nature of some of its attractions. Apart from museums dedicated to the world history of pairs of spectacles or packs of playing cards, you will also come across bars with a passion for one entirely ludicrous thing.

In this case it is donkeys.

The Ezeltje, or for fans of legendary Austrian singing duo Nina & Frederick "Little Donkey", is a small, one-roomed locals' bar situated just inside ring road on the way to Sint Pieters.

The bar is awash with pictures of donkeys and general donkey-abilila. At its far end is a fire to warm those donkeys on a cold winters night.

The donkey theme extends to the house beer, **Bassevelds Ezelsbier** (9%), a dry blond beer from Van Steenberge which is named after the inhabitants of the village of Bassevelde who are known, for reasons thankfully lost in history, as "the donkeys of Bassevelde".

Ganzespel 🍺 ✕ 🛋
37 Ganzestraat
☎ 050 33 12 33
www.ganzespel.be
🕐 Monday & Tuesday
🕕 18.00–22.00
🍴 22
🍴 Full restaurant menu, including local specialities and daily specials.

This tiny café restaurant is just around the corner from the Nieuw Museum and the Nisse (below) and thus a wee bit off the beaten track.

The "Goose Game" is housed in adjoining step-gabled buildings that also accommodate Nicky's Bed & Breakfast and below a two-roomed restaurant, one room of which is non-smoking

The restaurant has a small number of candlelit tables, which makes dining an intimate experience. Its menu is strong on local dishes and steaks, with an additional daily menu that offers exceptionally good value.

The beer menu is short and sweet, but does include a few gems. One of these is **Deugniet** (7.3%) a stronger blonde ale from the du Bocq brewery at Purnode,

in the Meuse valley of Namur province. Its name means Rascal in the Flemish dialect. The same beer sells as Triple Moine in the French-speaking parts of the country.

Garre

29 't Garre
1 De Garre
T 050 34 10 29
⊗ Last weeks of January & June
🍺 Sa 11.00–01.00; others 12.00–24.00
🍷 125
🥪 Sandwiches only

The business card says "De must in Brugge" and it is.

A *"garre"* is a tiny alley, typically forming an ancient fire escape. We have no reason to believe this *garre* is otherwise.

The small downstairs room is the epitome of elegant Bruges. The tiny staircase leads to an equally small balcony room upstairs. They will not let you stand and drink.

Your chosen beer is lovingly served on a tiny individual tray with a doily, and a tiny dish of cheese. Enjoy this to a background of Mozart. Ravel's Bolero played late at night means "Time, gentlemen please!"

A long-standing favourite of beer lovers round the globe, it a great café for its huge beer list alone (with no Pils!). Yet something about the ambience makes it the one that people often re-member with most nostalgia. ("Have you been to the one down that blind alley place?")

De Garre discourages intoxication in favour of sampling that which is different. **Witkap Stimulo** (6%), a refreshing, light blond ale from the Slaghmuylder family's brewery at Ninove, west of Brussels epitomises this ideal.

Gezelleke

AROUND BRUGES 30 IN 80 BEERS

't Gezelleke 🍷 ❌
15 Carmersstraat
☎ 050 33 83 81
www.chouffeclub.be
🕐 Sunday
🍷 Sa 16.00–02.00; Fr 11.00–02.00;
others to 24.00
22
🍴 Bar snacks including goat's cheese
croques and *vispannetje*.

The Gezelleke café could translate into English as the "Cosy Inn", though it also makes allusions to the Flemish poet Guido Gezelle, who lived round here. You will find it on the road that links the city centre to the windmills on the ring road, in what might be termed mews Bruges.

A pretty, old-style Flemish café with high ceilings and a black-and-white tiled floor, this cosy candlelit single roomed bar styles itself as an "eating and chatting" place.

The service is friendly. The owners are friends of Kris Bauweraerts who founded the Achouffe brewery near Houffalize in Luxembourg province, deep in the Ardennes. He sometimes sends kegs of his draught beer to the café.

Its beer list includes a number of 75cl bottles, not always a regular feature in Bruges. One of those is **McChouffe** (8.5%), Achouffe's dark ruby brown beer with a deep, slightly spicy, sweet taste that always delivers.

43

Goldies

31 Goldies 🍷
   18a Kerkstraat (Damme)
T 050 67 30 04
F 050 67 30 05
E info@goldies.be
   www.goldies.be
⊗ Thursday
🕐 From 11.00
🍸 33
🍴 Bar snacks including pasta,
   sandwiches and desserts

Goldies is a newly refurbished modern café right on the corner of Damme's Markt. The name is a condensation of Golden Oldies and the bar follows this theme with picture discs of earlier decades adorning the walls.

There are two separate bar rooms inside and a sizable drinking terrace out, with a great view of the square and the statue of Jacob van Maerlandt. He is seen as one of the greatest Flemish poets of the Middle Ages and resided in Damme during the 13th century.

As well as the famous Trappist beers, made under the control of real monks, Belgium makes a number of approved "abbey beers", brewed at the request or with the permission of various religious orders that benefit financially from their production. Belgium has about 70 such beers.

Ramée Blonde (8%) is one such. It is an unusual beer to find in Damme, being made for Jacques Mortelmans, who has led restoration of the spectacular buildings of Ramée abbey near Jodoigne, in Wallonian Brabant. It is brewed close to the French border in western Hainaut by Brunehaut brewery.

The beer is golden, bitter and slightly on the tart side.

De Gouden Aap 🍷 ✖

18 't Zand

T 050 33 48 48

Open all week

From 08.00

21

Full restaurant menu, including great salads.

Location, location, location. If you wait long enough all human life will pass your window at this café on 't Zand.

The Golden Ape *(Fr: Singe d'Or)* in question is the rather odd, long-legged golden monkey perched on the fireplace. This is the central focus of an attractive old café interior that also features much wood panelling and handpainted scenes.

At Christmas time they have the most beautifully decorated bar on the square, with a tree that has to be seen to be believed.

The featured beer here is **Corsendonk Agnus** (7.5%), brewed for a beer distributor in northern Antwerp by du Bocq brewery of Namur. This golden blonde beer has a rounded citrus, vanilla taste and is one of the most widely available "commissioned" beers in Belgium.

Corsendonk bier

33 Gran Kaffee de Passage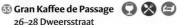
26–28 Dweersstraat
T 050 34 02 32
F 050 34 01 40
E info@passagebruges.com
www.passagebruges.com
⊗ mid-Jan to mid-Feb
🍷 Fr–Su 19.00–01.00; other to 24.00
🍺 27
🍽 Full restaurant menu, including some cooking with beer and a good vegetarian choice.

Dweersstraat links Noordzandstraat and Zuidzandstraat, off 't Zand. Here you will find this hotel, hostel, café and restaurant business trying hard to offer best value and high quality in all its many lines of work.

The main bar is decorated in the Art Deco *fin de siècle* grand café style. There are sumptuous cushions on the bench seating, where you can eat and sip your beer while staring at the giant stags' heads at the end of the bar.

Meals here are in what the Belgians call the Burgundian tradition, from the days when the Dukes of Burgundy ran the northern branch of the Hapsburg empire from various bases in what was then called the Low Countries.

The beer menu is marked up on huge wall mirrors and includes several beers from the St Bernardus brewery, set among the hopbines to the west of Poperinge, near the French border with West Flanders. **St Bernardus Pater** (6.5%) is luscious, fruity, dark brown and sweet.

36 Mariastraat
T 050 33 06 14
F 050 34 18 33
E Gruuthusehof@gruuthusehof.be
www.gruuthusehof.be
Wednesday & Thursday
10.00–21.30
14
Full restaurant menu,
including excellent fish

At the back of Simon Stevinplein, off Steenstraat, this easy-to-find restaurant looks out over the Maria Church. Its name refers to its former role as the place where the town's many small brewers came to buy *gruut*, a mix of herbs and spices added to beers as flavouring and preservatives. It has been run by three generations of the same family since 1955.

The big draw here is the classical Flemish cuisine, with their forte being fish dishes in all their simplicity and complexity. Expect to find creations based on all the Belgian coastal favourites such as sole (Du: *zeetong*), Trout (Du: *forel*), monkfish (Du: *zeeduivel*), mussels (Du: *mosselen*), salmon (Du: *zalm*) and tiny North Sea shrimps (Du: *garnalen*). There are meat and chicken dishes too.

This is one of the few establishments in Bruges that does not sell the ubiquitous Duvel. Instead they offer **Lucifer** (8.5%), brewed by Liefmans at Dentergem near Kortrijk.

This big straw-coloured beer with a rocky, fluffy white head has an innocent appearance but packs a mighty punch. Not exactly a Duvel clone, more of a tribute brand.

Halve Maan

35 **De Halve Maan** 🍺
26 Walplein
T 050 33 26 97
F 050 34 59 35
E info@halvemaan.be
www.halvemaan.be
Open all week
🕐 10.00–18.00
🍷 2
🍴 Bar meals

The smell of brewing is back in Bruges once more.

Prior to the First World War the city centre could once boast more than 30 breweries. At the start of the millennium there were still three breweries active. By 2004 there were none.

The Palm group decided to stop making beer at the Gouden Boom brewery in Langestraat after nearly six centuries of brewing on the site. The Brugse Bierkaai brewpub and microbrewery next to the Dijver canal, launched in 2000, failed to catch the imagination of either locals or tourists and soon went under.

Meanwhile, the old Halve Maan (Half Moon) brewery on Walplein was brewing the famous Straffe Hendrik beers. Although the brewery was still owned and managed by the descendents of its founder Henri Maes, the brewing, distribution and brands were all controlled by the Riva brewery. With investment needed at Halve Maan, Riva moved most of the brewing over to its bigger brewery at Dentergem, near Kortrijk.

By 2004 the city that had wooed a generation of foreign visitors round to the idea that Belgian beer was beautiful, had none to call its own. Only Johan

Brandt's excellent Regenboog brewery was technically within the city's domains but this was out in the suburb of Assebrook and Johan was already talking about taking the production of his beautifully hand-crafted beers to an expanded site near Oudenaarde in East Flanders.

Ironically, none of this stopped brewery companies wanting to associate their beers with beautiful Bruges. Beers continued to sport names and labels that gave the world the impression they were made in the city, even though some were coming from giant factories in France.

With Gouden Boom being measured up to become an apartment block, Halve Maan operating as a museum and Brugse Bierkaai folding, beer lovers assumed that beer-making in Bruges would be consigned to the history books. Indeed when we first heard that brewing was to restart at Halve Maan, it was assumed by some to be a spoof.

In fact, the spring of 2004 had seen Xavier Vanneste, son of Véronique Maes and great-great-great-grandson of Henri Maes qualify from brewing school in Ghent. He had already brewed an experimental blond beer at the Huyghe brewery near Ghent, which had been sold at the Halve Maan café and was well received. What better graduation present than for the family to decide to invest in new brewing equipment? An excellent career move for Xavier and the reinstatement of a great tradition for the company.

Although brewing had ceased, the Halve Maan had remained a successful business, with hordes of tourists still visiting the old brewery or simply enjoying the food at the café and, almost invariably, trying the Straffe Hendrik beers, albeit not made on the premises.

In 2004, Xavier made some test brews and asked the opinion of visitors to the tasting hall of Halve Maan. The views were duly noted and in 2005 a new beer was formally launched, called Brugse Zot. The name means "Bruges' Fool" and comes from the remark of Hapsburg Emperor Maximilian, who visited the city in the 15th century amid wild festivities. On being asked for funds to build a new lunatic asylum he suggested the whole place was one already.

You can either sit in the former bottling hall and enjoy a beer or a tasty meal from the menu of recommended beer cuisine. If you want to find out more about the history of the brewery you can for €4,50 join one of the 45-minute tours that depart on the hour every hour from 11.00 every day. The last tour is at 15.00 on weekdays (16.00 Apr-Oct), or 16.00 at weekends (17.00 Apr-Oct).

Brugse Zot Blond (6%) is their first beer though even this one is still developing. It is an easy-drinking, likeable brew that even those used only to lagers should be able to understand.

Hof van Rembrandt

36 't Hof van Rembrandt
10 Eiermarkt
T 050 33 74 50
www.hofvanrembrant.be
Open all week
From 11.00
28
Bar snacks including pasta,
omelettes and salads

The Rembrandt's Court is found in the old Egg Market, a small square off the main Markt, which is packed with more youthful bars that stay open into the early hours.

In summer its trade comes from its large umbrella-clad sun terrace, while in winter the bar has an open fire for night-time huddling.

Food is incidental here and runs to spaghetti with various sauces, baguettes, omelettes and salads.

Although the beer menu is relatively short it has some real treats. For example there are La Chouffe and Chimay Triple on draught and a fine selection of Trappist beers. One of these comes from the newest monastery to open a brewery, the cloister at Achel.

The abbey of St. Benedict is bang on the Dutch border at the northernmost tip of Limburg province, in a delightfully rustic setting best reached by cycling the wooded roads from the nearby village. Its brewhouse opened in 1999, when it joined the exclusive group of brewers who make beer that can be sold as an Authentic Trappist Product.

Achel Blond (8%) is an approachable straw-coloured beer with a good hop balance, which continues to gain class with the passage of the years.

Hollandse Vismijn

Hollandse Vismijn
4 Vismarkt
T 050 33 33 01
Tuesday
From 08.00
27
None

Holland is that part of the western Netherlands that stretches from the delta of the river Schelde to the old Zuiderzee, now the Ijsselmeer lake. Whether it has any fish mines is open to question.

This Hollandse Vismijn looks out onto Bruges' fish market (Du: *vismarkt*), appropriately still held several days a week on the square that takes its name.

Defiantly against an onslaught of international tourism, the fishers ply their trade, selling mainly to local Brugeans, who feel this is still their part of town. Here the language spoken is predominantly Flemish rather than the myriad of languages you will usually hear elsewhere.

The bar expresses its political leanings in its décor, with a red rose stained glass panel and photographs of local politicians. Beats horse brasses anyway. It is good to get away from tourist prices too.

There is a heated terrace for those who like to be toasted on chill winter evenings. This doubles as the sun terrace in warmer months.

The bar has that most Flemish of West Flanders beers, **Rodenbach** (5%) on draught. This is the version that is a blend of plain brown ale with beer aged in oak for two years. It is the biggest selling beer of the style in Belgium. Its slightly sour taste is deliberate and comes from the ageing. The sharper it gets, the more thirst quenching and palate-cleansing it is.

38 Huyze Die Maene
17 Markt
T 050 33 39 59
F 050 33 44 60
E huyzediemaene@pandora.be
www.huyzediemaene.be
Open all week
🕐 09.00–23.00
🍷 25
🍽 Full restaurant menu,
including breakfasts

Although the view of Bruges' old market square from the terraces of the café-restaurants that line it is probably one of the finest urban vistas in Europe, it usually comes at a price.

The bars and restaurants on the "famous for being famous" Markt are pricier than almost everywhere else in Bruges. Some add insult to injury by offering very limited beer menus and ridiculous prices but others manage to have a couple of decent beers at prices that won't make you scream.

This handsome café, which now sports a restaurant and small luxury hotel too, offers the chance of a great view with an affordable beer. The city's famous horse-drawn carriages ply their trade directly in front of the terrace. In colder weather the retreat indoors reveals pleasantly elegant décor.

Breakfast is served from 09.00 to 11.00. All day long, good food is based on seasonal availability of ingredients. The menu is in several languages.

One of the beers on draught here is **Brugge Blond** (6.5%) from Palm brewery in Steenhuffel. Although in the English-speaking world such a beer would be considered strong, in Belgium this would be considered a decent workaday light drinking beer with a touch of hoppiness.

Jerry's Cigar Bar
13 Simon Stevinplein
T 050 33 77 94
F 050 33 77 94
E info@jerrycigarbar.com
www.jerrycigarbar.com
Open all week
Sa&Su 09.00–19.00; others 08.00–19.00
12
None

Don't tell them in California, New York, Ireland or the UK but some countries actually have bars that encourage people to smoke. Jerry's is an incredibly well-stocked cigar shop with stoggies from all over the world and a cosy modern bar attached at the rear. The place is well worth a visit even if you don't smoke cigars, but a paradise for those who do.

The bar is on in the corner of a small square, halfway along Steenstraat between 't Zand and Markt, opposite the sidestreet that is home to Brugs Beertje (above). The amazing variety of cigars stored in the humidors all around the shop are enough to make you want to take up smoking as a new obsession. Watching Americans worry about whether they should try the Cubans is a hoot.

The menu offers a Balmoral cigar and the drink of the week, a coffee cognac matched with its own cigar or a Karmeliet and a Cohiba.

The bar stocks beers from the Bosteels brewery in Buggenhout, northwest of Brussels and features **Karmeliet Tripel** (8%).

The distinguishing feature of this strong blond ale is that it is brewed using three grains – unmalted wheat, malted oats and malted barley. The result is a really charcterful, superb *tripel* that leans towards sweetness and is certainly moreish.

Kelk

40 De Kelk 🍷
69 Langestraat
T 0473 73 34 60
www.dekelk.be
⊗ Monday
🕐 From 17.00
🍷 80+
🍴 *Crôques* only.

Ah! The Chalice.

This dark candle-lit place, awash with Champagne paraphernalia, sports one of those lengthy beer lists where not all the stock is available at any given time, so have a list of reserve choices ready.

Although it is aimed at younger drinkers, old farts are welcome and can usually remember the words and music better for having been there when they first came out. The place is laid back if he likes you Zucchero the deaf Dalmatian will lounge lumpenly at your feet and sniff.

The beer menu manages to feature twenty-four fruit beers avoiding anything decent. On the up side there is an impressive range of more than thirty official abbey beers, used subtly to massage the younger clientele into a greater appreciation of fine ales. There is certainly a move towards beer education – watch this space.

There will always be beers from De Dolle Brouwers in stock. This excellent brewery, bought in 1980 by the extraordinary Hertelaer family has been a real inspiration to the Belgian brewing scene since they first stuck a bow tie on a bottle quarter of a century ago. All their beers are worth seeking out and here we suggest **Arabier** (7%) the pale, dry-hopped beer, full of character with a white fluffy head.

33 CL. ℮
℮0,10
CAT. S
ara bier
BREWED & BOTTLED BY
DE DOLLE BROUWERS IN
8600 ESEN BELGIUM

De Kleine Nachtmuziek
60 Sint Jakobsstraat
T 050 33 50 84
Wednesday
From 18.00
32
Light snacks only (to 02.00)

Cosy, laid back café with a Sydney Greenstreet fan and two pianos used as room dividers. There is much Guinness and whisky memorabilia along with candlelight and friendly service. Despite the name of the café the music leans more towards blues and folk, with very little night music from Mozart.

lambic beers, and traditional gueuze in particular, this is a beer that will require you to suspend everything you have learnt about beer thus far.

Oude gueuze is unique to Brussels and the Payottenland area to its West. Matured in oak casks for years, after being fermented by wild yeast from the atmosphere. The versions from the Drie Fonteinen brewery at Beersel are sometimes equalled, rarely bettered.

Impossible, absurd and quite unlike any other form of drink you will ever encounter. Finest dry cider meets extract of aged burgundy against a vaguely grainy backdrop. Expect to hate your first one but be tempted back for a second nonetheless.

The menu is a lever arch file and features huge quantities of whiskies from Scotland, Ireland and the USA. The beer menu is also fairly strong and has the complete range of beers from the Roman brewery of Oudenaarde in East Flanders, including Ename Blonde and Dubbel on draught.

However, the one beer that stands out above all others is **Drie Fonteinen Oude Gueuze** (6%), one of the best lambic beers of all. If you have not tried

42 **De Kluiver** 🍷
12 Hoogstraat
T 050 33 89 27
E hendrik@dekluiver.be
www.dekluiver.be
⊗ Tuesday & Wednesday
🕐 Th from 18:00; others from 16.00
🍸 20
🍴 Bar snacks such as quiches, pasta and meatballs.

A *kluiver* is the Dutch name for a particular sail on a sailboat and is the theme for this small cosy bistro-bar, just off Burg. So for example the ceiling is dressed in billowing canvas and there is a serious collection of biscuit tins and tea caddies featuring sailing boats on the walls.

The food menu also features a dish of the day and if you are really lucky/curious/ up for anything, try the hot whelks.

The beer we feature here is the Belgian Trappist classic, Orval, from the abbey of Orval near Florenville in one of the most attractive parts of the Ardennes, in Luxembourg province.

The design on the bottle is derived from the legend that Mathilda of Tuscany visited the construction site of the first monastery in 1076. On putting her hands into a nearby spring, the wedding ring given to her by her late husband slipped off and fell into the lake.

After praying for its return, a trout is said to have appeared on the surface of the water with the ring in its mouth and they all lived happily ever after.

Whatever you think of the story, **Orval** (6.2%) is certainly a legendary beer. Orangey-amber in colour, with an intense, hoppy bitterness and a long dry finish it gets even better when aged in the cellar for a year or more.

De Kogge
7 Braambergstraat
T 0474 69 56 03
Sunday, Monday & public holidays
Sa 16.30–20.00;
others 16.30–01.00
27
None

In the days of the Hanseatic league, Bruges was one of the great trading cities of Europe. Much of the merchandise destined for Bruges arrived by sea at the port of Damme in a cargo boat known as a *kogge*.

The café that takes its name is said to be the smallest in Bruges and has a charm like no other. Because of its size there is little room to move, although you can often get a stool at the bar.

The history of the place can be traced back to the 17th century when custody of the building passed from the Guild of Tanners to the Guild of Grain Carriers – captured by the 1637 carvings outside. This was the trade centre for the transportation of grain for the whole of Bruges.

This old Brugean house is mainly a locals bar but passing tourists are made welcome. The walls are covered in work by local artists. There are a couple of small tables on the galleried first floor with a great view below.

Like the café, the beer list is small but impressive with the amazing Saison Dupont and beers from the highly respected Malheur brewery of Buggenhout, northwest of Brussels. One of those beers is **Malheur 12** (12%) a big strong warming barley wine – just the thing for a rainy autumn evening.

Kuppe

44 De Kuppe
19 Kuipersstraat
T 050 33 39 20
Open all week
🕐 Sa&Su from 14.00; others from 11.00
🍺 80+
🍴 None

You will find this strangely incongruous café just behind the Opera House, not far off Markt.

By day this is a pleasant quiet place to call for a couple of beers but at night it springs to life and then carries on into the wee small hours. The area round Kuiperstraat has a few late night bars, something not so common in the centre of Bruges.

The Kuppe certainly has a wide choice of quality beers at some of the best prices in town. It advertises a hundred but is another place where not all are in stock, so it is best to have your reserve list ready.

Here is a good place to try **Rodenbach Grand Cru** (6.5%), one of Belgium's most remarkable beers. This starts life as a regular brown ale but is then matured in huge oak tuns in a massive fermentation hall for up to two years. It is then matched and blended to create a spritzy, tangy beer that is quintessentially Flemish.

Grand Cru has to be tasted to be believed. It is a hugely sophisticated beer that is often popular with lovers of fine red wines.

5 Lamme Goedzak
31 Noorweegse Kaai
T 050 28 86 10 (Damme Tourism)
October to March
From Bruges 10.00, 12.00, 14.00, 16.00 &
18.00; from Damme 9.15, 11.00, 13.00,
15.00 & 17.20
15
None

One of the more novel places to drink quality beer is on board the good ship Lamme Goedzak, which spends half the year ploughing backwards and forwards along the seven kilometres of canal between Bruges and Damme.

It is known as the Napoleon canal as it was built in 1810 by Spanish prisoners of war on the orders of Napoleon.

The pick up point at the Bruges end is just outside the ring road beyond Dampoort. This can be reached by the number 43 bus from Markt and 't Zand and if you have missed the boat, carries on to Damme itself!

The boat makes its way more sedately and completes the pleasant journey in just over half an hour. Naturally the boat has a bar on board for you to while away the journey to Damme with a beer in hand. Most of these are from the country's oldest family brewery, Roman, founded in 1515 and boasts some twelfth generation family members on its Board.

Their **Ename Tripel** (9%) is typically strong, packed with flavour, light in colour from using Pilsener malt and refermented in the bottle.

46 Eetcafé Leopold 🍺
26 't Zand
T 050 33 19 87
⊗ Wednesday & Thursday
🕐 From 10.00
🍸 40
🍴 Small snacks only

The modern kingdom of Belgium was created at the London Conference of 1830. Its first king, Leopold I, was first married to the daughter of the English King George IV, who would have ascended the British throne had she not died after a miscarriage in 1821.

Leopold had fought at Waterloo and during his 35-year reign created a country that developed so rapidly and confidently that its progress continued despite the reign of his son, Leopold II, the only monarch of recent times to take a country (Congo) as his personal fiefdom.

Anyway, this family-run bar with its splendid view of the new concert hall, is a shrine to all things Leopold. Owner Alain Talloen is proud of his impressive collection of enamel signs featuring the beers that Belgium has named after its favourite King, some over 70 years old.

Unusually for Belgium, the café has a no smoking area where nobody actually smokes.

The beer menu is a model of clarity with a picture of each bottle and glass alongside tasting notes and the strength of each beer.

Our chosen beer here is **La Chouffe** (8%), the most successful beer from the most successful of the newer Wallonian breweries, Achouffe of Luxembourg province. The easy-drinking appeal of this strong blonde ale comes from the coriander that is mixed into the brew.

— LA —
CHOUFFE
Blonde d'Ardenne

www.achouffe.be

47 Lokkedize 🍷 ✗
33 Korte Vulderstraat
T 050 33 44 50
E letsgobruges@skynet.be
✗ Monday & Tuesday
From 18.00
🍷 18
Full restaurant menu,
including Greek cuisine

Slightly off the beaten track, though it is only one block off Zuidzandstraat between Steenstraat and 't Zand. "Hard to find – worth the discovery" says its blurb, and we would agree.

Its attractive candlelit interior has exposed brick walls on which musical instruments are displayed everywhere. The service is fast and friendly and the atmosphere is convivial.

The menu is very Greek island, with retsina, tsatsiki, feta salad, taramaslata and calamari all on there.

Although this is a restaurant it is enough of a café to stay open unusually late and expect customers whose main interest is late beers. The kitchen stays open till late (01.00 Fr&Sa; 24.00 others).

Unsurprisingly Moortgat brewery's top-selling **Duvel** (8.5%) is available here, as it is in the vast majority of bars in Bruges. This is the beer that defined the style of the strong golden ale. And thus far at least the commercial success of the family-influenced, publicly quoted Moortgat brewery has not caused it to compromise the quality of its flagship product.

In its distinctive glass this straw coloured spritzy beer goes from strength to strength, and long may it do so.

Lunatic

48 Lunatic 🍷 ✕
11 Kuipersstraat
T 050 34 08 00
www.gotolunatic.be
✕ Tuesday
🌙 Mo 11.00–17.00; Su from 15.00;
others from 11.00
🍷 24
🍴 Full restaurant menu,
changing with the seasons

Another of those late night bistro-cafés on Kuipersstraat, this one taking on a moon theme. Its bendy bar snakes through the room and extends into the restaurant at its rear.

The kitchen likes to experiment a bit with menu regular food themed evenings based on seasonal dishes. Which is not to say that it averse to serving up loads of half-a-chicken with *frites*, giant kebabs, Thai curries and fish dishes.

Our featured beer here is Van Honsebrouck brewery's **Kasteelbier Bruin** (11%). Ever a brewery with an eye to the main chance, it first produced a blond and brown version of its "Castle Beer" in 1989. The family's own castle is pictured on the bottle labels and the handsome chalice glass in which this beer is served.

Whatever you think of Kasteelbier Donker, subtlety is not a word that comes to mind. Sweetness pervades this uncompromising experience, which some adore.

9 The Meeting 🍷 ✕ 🍽️
Relais Oud Huis Amsterdam
3 Spiegelrei
T 050 34 18 10
www.oha.be
Open all week
From 16.30
12
Full restaurant menu, in the main hotel

Now for a slice of luxury.

The Meeting is the name of the first class hotel bar, entered from Genthof, of the restored 17th century gentlemen's houses now called the Relais Oud Huis Amsterdam Hotel.

It is open to all, service is so good you feel genuinely loved and the roaring fires and fresh flowers on the table make you feel pretty special too.

Relax in an armchair, lean back, sip your St Bernardus and watch the firelight glint off the copper and brass pots all around. Remind us to stay here when we launch our sixth edition – the one with the interactive holographs.

It is nowhere near as unusual nowadays to find top quality beers at top quality hotels. Here **St Bernardus Abt 12** (10%) really catches the mood. Its mahogany-hued glow and warming brandy richness adds to the fireside enjoyment.

Napoleon

50 Pub Napoleon
1 Hoogste van Brugge
T 0486 87 85 67
⊗ Tuesday
🍷 From 19.00
🍷 27
🍷 None

Off the top end of Zuidzandstraat just
before it hits 't Zand is this small street
corner café where everybody gathers
round the central bar. Just off the main
tourist drag but a world away too.
Darts is the game of choice here and
the players can get quite excitable.

We assume that if it ever got seriously
out of hand Napoleon himself would be
called on to intervene – he's the Boxer
dog behind the bar.

This is an ideal place for a nightcap
and what fills the bill better than
Rochefort 10 (11.3%). The profits from
the sale of Rochefort beers are all
ploughed back into the upkeep of the
abbey, the Order and the good causes it
supports.

This deep and delectable black-brown
barley wine should be sipped and
savoured. Rochefort is another of the six
Trappist breweries of Belgium, based at
an abbey near the market town of
Rochefort in Namur province.

NieuwMuseum

In 't Nieuw Museum 🍷 ❌

42 Hooistraat

050 33 12 80

050 33 12 22

www.nieuwmuseum.be

Monday

Sa & Su from 12.00–14.00 & 18.00;
others from 18.00

50

Bar meals, including steaks and
seafood grilled over the open fire

smell of it cooking while Murphy, the ginger cat, looks on. He is very friendly, particularly if you order the seafood.

This is one of the few cafes in town to carry the two Oxfam beers. They also stock **St. Feuillien Blonde** (7.5%) a dry, hoppy, golden brew which is very drinkable. The beer for these smaller bottles is actually brewed at du Bocq in Namur. The draught version and any in large (1.5 litre) bottles is made at the family-run St. Feuillien brewery at Le Roeulx, between Mons and Charleroi.

It is well worth the extra walk along the canals out of the town centre to find this one. Go on – walk off a few of those pancakes!

Great food and beer combine to make this a great family-run café. So much so that a new room has been has been built to accommodate the overflow.

Many of the people who come here have been drawn by the spectacular grills, cooked over the huge open fire in the middle of the bar. Order a beer, then order your mixed grill and enjoy the

St Feuillien
anno 1125
Bière d'abbaye   Abdijbier
Blonde   Blond

52 De Nisse ✕
   12 Hooistraat
T 050 34 86 51
F 050 34 86 51
✕ Tuesday & Wednesday
🕐 Sa&Su from 12.00; others from 18.00
🍷 14
🍴 Full restaurant menu, including
   excellent fish dishes and fondues

This restaurant in the same street as the previous entry, is under new management.

The house dates from 1583 and is found in the same characterful street as the previous entry. It is called "Nisse" after the small niche above the door, which holds a little weathered stone bear, the symbol of Bruges.

The food here is highly recommended. They pride themselves on their scampi and fish dishes, thought their house special is fondue. Four varieties of meat are served with sauces, chips and bread. It works best if there is a group of you.

Reservations are requested as this is mainly a restaurant though at quieter times you can just grab a beer. They will open at lunchtime for large parties. There is a beautiful enclosed garden terrace out back.

The beer of choice here is **Rochefort 8** (9.2%), the mostly commonly found beer from the Trappist abbey at Rochefort. This beer is not on the official menu but is available to nthose who ask. It has been described as liquid bread and certainly mops up the juices from a T-bone steak.

d' Oude Speye
7 Kerkstraat (Damme)
0474 41 26 57
www.oudespeye.be
Monday & Tuesday (Sep–Jun)
Jul & Aug from 09.00; others from 12.00
210
Only *croques*

On the corner of the main village square of Damme, a short walk from where the Lamme Goedzak moors (see above). Parts of the building date from the 13th century though it has only been a pub for four hundred years or so.

Outside the front of the café there is a small drinking terrace on the cobbles. Inside is a large, square, high-ceilinged room with comfortable sofas and a relaxing atmosphere.

The beer list runs to well over 200 and is particularly strong on Trappist beers, wheat beers, *gueuze* and *kriek*. Owner Phillippe used to work in the brewery trade before coming to the café in June 2003 and is an expert on lambic beers.

He runs beer tastings and will gear a tasting to your personal preferences.

It would be churlish not to choose a lambic beer here, so why not go for **De Cam Oude Kriek** (6.5%). When De Cam started storing and blending lambic beers at Gooik in Payottenland in 1997 they were the first new lambic blenders for two generations.

Their Oude Kriek is made by the traditional method of stepping whole cherries in lambic beer, in oak casks, for a full six months. When newly bottled the colour is almost blood red with a pink head. The taste is a beautiful compromise of sharp and sour lambic with full, dry cherry fruit flavour.

Oxfam Wereldwinkel

54 Oxfam Wereldwinkel 🛒
8 Geldmuntstraat
T 050 33 11 68
F 050 34 33 90
E brugge@oww.be
www.oww.be
Open all week
🕐 Sa from 10.00–18.00;
others from 9.00–12.30 & 13.30–18.00
🍷 2
🍴 For self-catering only

Oxfam shops in Belgium are different from British ones. Instead of selling second hand clothes they are called Worldshops because they concentrate on selling new products sourced from individuals and small groups around the world. They concentrate on Fair Trade and organic produce, which the Belgians call "bio".

This shop is to be found on the less populated of the two shopping streets that link 't Zand and Markt. Items on offer include small household goods, clothes, toys and jewellery.

They also sell food and drink products such as rice, spices, teas, coffees, wine, and two specially brewed bottled beers.

They are both brewed at the Huyghe brewery at Melle, near Ghent. One contains quinoa from Bolivia, the other basmati rice from India and cane sugar from Costa Rica. As a world expert in all things beery you are bound to know that quinoa is a type of seed that has recently been "rediscovered" as a potentially useful nutrient and ingredient. It has a light, delicate taste and is used in the mash for **Oxfam Blond** (7.5%), beer with a light orangey colour and an interesting but sweet taste.

't Pallieterke 🍷 🍴

28 't Zand
050 34 01 77
050 34 01 77
pallieterke1@telenet.be
www.pallieterke.com
Monday & Tuesday
11.30–21.30
17
Full restaurant menu, including rabbit with prunes, mussels, fish *waterzooi*, carbonade of beef and others

A typical 't Zand café-restaurant, with a restaurant at the back of an all-year-round front-facing conservatory, appropriately heated in the winter.

Here you are treated to a full frontal view of that new concert hall – so bring your Ray-Bans.

Full meals are available throughout opening hours and those ubiquitous waffles, pancakes and ice creams can be ordered between 14.00 and 18.00 should you be feeling peckish.

The outstanding beer on this restaurant menu is **St Bernardus Tripel** (8%) from Watou. This brewery was originally set up in 1946 to brew imitation Trappist beers at the request of the monks at St Sixtus' abbey at Westvleteren, which did not have the capacity to go commercial in any serious way.

Iin 1992 the Order took back their licence, leaving the brewery without any brands. They responded by improving the existing imitations and then adding some new beers. The Tripel was the first of these and became an instant success, giving the Trappist breweries a run for their money by creating a beer with an excellent balance of malt and hop character.

Panier d'Or

56 Le Panier d'Or
28 Markt
T 050 34 32 34
F 050 34 60 09
www.restaurant-tompouce.be
Open all week
From 09.00
5
Full restaurant menu, with lobster the speciality of the house

The Golden Basket sits in an unbroken row of cafes on one side of the square, facing the belfry. It is possibly the most photographed café in Europe since the invention of the camera.

Like all cafés on this famous square, it is quite expensive, but its great view of the leaning Belfry tower, particularly splendid when lit up at night, is worth a bit extra.

Incidentally the climb up the tower is 366 steps to a panoramic take on the city and in fine weather a view to the coast 12 km away. You can also see the clock mechanism close up, and if you are really lucky the 47-bell carillon will burst your ear drums while you are up there.

The cafes on Markt generally offer unchallenging, bland beers from global corporations. However, Panier d'Or is unusual in offering draught **Pauwel Kwak** (8%) from the Bosteels brewery, served in it's the round-bottomed coachman's glass with a wooden stand, which made its name. The beer is a malty amber ale that errs on the side of sweetness.

Kaffee Pergola 🍴 ✕ 🛏
Steenhouwersdijk/Meestraat
050 44 76 50
050 33 66 74
pergola@dieswaene.com
www.dieswaene.com
Open all week
Tu&We 11.30–15.00; others 11.30–21.00
8
Full restaurant menu with
an array of delicate eats

The Pergola is the café of the prestigious hotel, Die Swaene. A member of the Small Luxury Hotels of the World Group and genuinely an extremely fine small hotel, the Swan has been used as a backdrop in many films and TV-productions. Enjoy a bistro lunch, afternoon tea or an aperitif before dinner while the canal craft chug by the garden. The hotel's glass-walled structure affords views of the surrounding buildings and the well-appointed garden.

Bearing in mind that they have a proper restaurant for serious dining, the Pergola has to make do with a menu that includes sautéed goose liver with apple or scallops with endive and curry sauce, followed by poached ray with capers or coivet of wild hare.

This is a really classy joint with fresh flowers on the table and top class service. Beers are served with a long ceramic tray containing a selection of exotic nuts, raisins, and a variety of other crunchy appetisers.

But the point is that nowadays top hotels stock some top quality beers and here you should try the sharp but smooth **Boon Oude Geuze** (7%) brewed at the Boon brewery in Lembeek, south of Brussels. This dry but mellow, unfiltered brew is at the heavier end of the lambic based beers. It comes in a corked 37.5cl bottle and is served and presented at the Pergola with appropriate ceremony.

Pietje Pek

58 **Pietje Pek** ⊗
 13 Sint Jakobsstraat
T 050 34 78 74
F 050 34 47 31
www.pietjepek.com
⊗ Wednesday
🕐 Su from 12.00–15.00 & 17.30;
 others from 17.30
🍸 5
🍽 Full restaurant menu, including regional
 Flemish cooking and fondues

This popular restaurant, not too far off Markt, has disabled facilities and is family-friendly. While younger ones are helping Jonas the rabbit find his way through the maze to the carrot, you can peruse the menus on the large blackboards, which your waiter will bring to your table in your preferred language.

The menu majors in fine Flemish cuisine. Why not try the North Sea shrimp croquettes as a starter, followed by a chicken or fish *waterzooi*, *Vlaamse carbonnade* (Flemish beef stew) or wild Cabourg rabbit *(sic)* marinated in Westmalle Dubbel.

Pietje Pek is also known for its house fondue with steak, veal and turkey, and its Swiss cheese fondue featuring a vat of melted Emmental, Gruyère, white wine and herbs with a dash of Kirsch and smoked ham on the side.

Although it is not as exclusive to the restauarant as they suggest, Pietje Pek is one of very few places in the city to serve **Westmalle Dubbel** (7%) on draught. The abbey at Westmalle, east of Antwerp, houses the most commercially adept of the Flemish Trappist breweries and its reddish-brown, full, fruity ale is one to be praised.

Republiek

De Republiek
36 Sint Jakobsstraat
050 34 02 29
050 33 06 97
info@derepubliek.be
www.derepubliek.be
Open all week
From 11.00
40
Full restauarant menu,
featuring world cooking

The Republic is home to the Theatre de Korre, the Cinema Lumière and the Cactus café. The last of these is a huge one-roomed bar with a large raised seating area and a feel of Students' Union meets American diner.

If you don't like the bar there is a large wall-enclosed gravel terrace at the rear, set around a circular tower. Relaxed but busy, with fast, efficient service, it seems to be popular with families and groups of all ages.

There is an impressive, detailed menu of international cuisine from Irish rib-eye steaks to wok-fried dishes, sashimi, chilli, enchiladas, chicken tikka, nachos and couscous.

There areplenty of new world wines and alcohol-free cocktails, plus an above average beer list.

The beer that stands out is **Grottenbier** (6.5%), brewed at St Bernardus brewery to the instructions of brewing legend Pierre Celis, the man who can claim to have brought wheat beer back to the world. It is named after the underground cave complex (Du. *grotten*) of Kanne, by the Dutch border near Maastricht, where the larger 75cl bottles are aged. Complex and herbal, its luxuriant woody, resiny flavour suggests it is stronger than it is.

Schrijverke

60 'tSchrijverke ✕
    4 Gruuthusestraat
T 050 33 29 08
E tschrijverke@pandora.be
   www.tschrijverke.be
✕ Tuesday
🕙 10.00–22.00
🍷 25
🍴 Full restaurant menu

Set in the shadow of the 122-metre high tower of the Church of our Lady, not far from the Groeninge Museum, this nice little restaurant takes its name from one of the poems of Guido Gezelle, a 19th century son of Bruges, commemorated in stone nearby.

The specialities of the house are its mussels (in season) and cooking with beer. One particular favourite is the duck breast in *frambozen* (raspberry beer), which as good as anything you will find in the city.

The beer menu is strong on beers from Van Steenberge but also carries the recently redesigned Brugge Tripel. The forerunner to this beer used to come from the Gouden Boom brewery in Langestraat, which also housed a brewing and malting museum. The old brewhouse is destined to become housing, with the contents of the brewery museum now moved to the Halve Maan brewery.

Brugge Tripel (8.2%) is a strong, sweet, amber beer, maltier than the average tripel, nowadays brewed at the Palm brewery in the village of Steenhuffel, in Flemish Brabant.

Smatch

Smatch 🛒
55 Langestraat
050 33 82 36
Sunday
08.30–19.30
85
For self-catering only

Yes, OK, so this is a supermarket. But with nearly half of beer in Belgium now being drunk at home and most of that coming from supermarkets, where is the big surprise?

What makes Smatch stand out in Bruges is that it has the largest range of beers of any supermarket in the city, and to their credit the range is ever-changing.

One apparently permanent feature is the beers of the Maredsous range, brewed by Moortgat, the makers of Duvel.

These official abbey beers are brewed in collaboration with the abbey of Maredsous in a beautiful part of Namur province, to the west of the river Meuse as it rolls through the northern reaches of the Ardennes.

Although most cafés in Bruges sell Duvel, few seem to stock these equally impressive beers. Although all are worth sampling, we have chosen the lightest, **Maredsous 6** (6%). The innocent of the range, this blonde, grainy bottle-conditioned beer is remarkably thirst-quenching and a good summer beer.

62 **Snuffel**
47–49 Ezelstraat
T 050 33 31 33
F 050 33 32 50
E info@snuffel.be
www.snuffel.be
Open all week
From 10.00
25
Toasties only

Snuffel is a backpacker hostel and together with Bauhaus (above) they are on the backpacker trail where information is swapped by world travellers.

They claim to have the cheapest everything in town – beds, beer, bikes and internet access. The bar is small and basic and is decorated with posters for bands and music. The obligatory collection of banknotes also makes an appearance. The music is wide-ranging and not over-loud.

They have a choice of thirty different board games. The internet corner and travellers library are well-used. English newspapers and magazines can also be found. Food is minimal. Fair trade coffee from Oxfam is available as are their two beers.

The beer list is on a board behind the bar and features **Delirium Tremens** (9%) from the Huyghe brewery near Ghent. The packaging is jokey, its stone-effect bottle bearing a label featuring pink elephants, dancing crocodiles and dragons on a balancing ball. Yet this is quite a serious beer full of fruit and heavy spice flavours and a warming, long, sweet afterglow.

63 De Stoepa 🍷 ⊗
  124 Westmeers
T 050 33 04 54
E info@stoepa.be
  www.stoepa.be
⊗ Monday
🕐 Su 13.00–15.00 & 18.00–24.00;
  others 12.00–14.00 & 18.00–24.00
🍺 22
🍴 Full restaurant menu,
  featuring Eastern specialities

On the back road from the station to 't Zand, this oriental café-restaurant is an unusual find for Bruges. As a general rule, the city does not do Eastern food to anywhere near the same degree that most international cites do nowadays.

Stoepa is the Flemish version of the word "stupa", as in Buddhist religious building. This is reflected in the cooking here, where there is a little bit of East meets West.

There are many Oriental specialities including rice, noodle and wok dishes but there are also the ever present pasta and shrimp croquettes. There is a great atmosphere to the place and the large terrace garden at the rear can really buzz in summer.

For a beer, why not try the **Brugse Straffe Hendrik Bruin** (8.5%), which originated at the Halve Maan brewery when it was brewing for Riva, now the Liefmans group. Nowadays this deep, rich, strong, polished brown ale in the abbey mould comes from Liefmans brewery at Dentergem near Kortrijk.

Stokershuis

64 't Stokershuis
7 Langestraat
T 050 33 55 88
⊗ Tuesday & Wednesday
From 18.30
23
Light snacks only

The Distiller's House is a smallish one-roomed café with a traditional Flemish feel. Candles light the pannelled walls, which are decorated with Delft tiles and Brugean artwork. Its attractive stone fireplace is typical of Bruges, with a husband and wife head at each end, holding up the mantlepiece.

There is spaghetti and a few other pasta snacks but this is primarily a place for liquid refreshment. As you would expect given its name, there is a good selection of quality genevers, the Belgian form of what the Dutch call *jenever*, the French call *genièvre* and the English call gin.

The Stokershuis also has on offer three of Liefmans most popular beers. These are the aged brown beer Goudenband and the two fruit beers based on rapberry (*framboos*) and cherry (*krieken*). All these beers come in 37.5cl bottles that are paper-wrapped.

Liefmans Goudenband (8%) is made from a blend of young and older beer, which is then bottled and left to referment in the brewery cellars for a time. Previous owners of the brewery had started to try to achieve these effects biochemically but a recent takeover has seen the welcome return of more traditional "slow beer" methods.

Goudenband is a dark reddish brown beer that tastes slightly caramelled with some fruity tartness in the background.

Strijdershuis 🍷 ✖
14 Hallestraat
T 050 61 62 60
www.hotel-koffieboontje.be/Resto/nl/
base_nl.htm
Open all week
Fr&Sa 10.00–1.00; others 10.00–24.00
40
Full restaurant menu including
a modern take on Flemish cuisine

Strijdershuis is on the corner of Oude Burg and Hallestraat, directly by the right side of the Belfry building as you face it from Markt. It is owned by the same people as the Koffieboontje Hotel, Witte Raaf restaurant and the bike hire shop, all in the same street.

This spacious and attractive modern two-floored bar with a non-smoking mezzanine opened for the first time late 2002 and eschewed all pretensions of doing 21st centrury Baroque, though there are vague Art Deco references here and there.

The food is varied with lots of reasonably priced daily specials. The scampi in a cream sauce, duck breast with vegetables and various versions of mussels have all been found to be outstanding. There is a good selection of South African wines too.

The beer list concentrates on particular breweries and despite the fact they usually have the full ranghe of Dolle Brouwers' beers here, we have chosen one from another of West Flanders' well respected family breweries, Strubbe. One of their best brews is **Vlaskop** (5.5%), a wheat beer brewed with a large amount of unmalted barley, which makes it drier and less cloudy than typical Belgian white beers.

Tempelier

66 De Tempelier
120 Gistelsesteenweg
T 0497 46 86 92
⊗ Sunday & Monday
🕐 Sa from 10.00; others from 16.00
🍷 20
🍴 None

Travel is a human game; discovery is its prize. To discover the Tempelier you need to travel the wrong way, taking unpromising Smedenstraat out of town from 't Zand towards the railway tracks. It should take you eight minutes on foot.

Entering from the street you will see nothing more unnerving that a good local pub with perhaps an above-average interest in pub games such as bar billiards and table football. But ask for a game of arrows and they will not hand you the darts. Instead, at the back you will find an

archery lane with all its fittings. And if that does not suit, it can convert into a Flemish style bowling alley.

The Tempelier is a real community pub or *lokaal*, untainted by tourism. In Belgium, these are often meeting places for local clubs and this place is HQ for an archery club, cycling club, darts club, football club, country dancing group and the local philatelists.

They also sport a pretty good beer menu, which has brews from West Flanders' Van Eecke and Leroy breweries and Wallonian Brabant's Lefèbvre.

Lefèbvre's signature beer is **Barbār** (8%), a pale honey beer in which the first hit is alcohol, followed by some of the subtler honey flavours. Manages to be sweet without being cloying. Worth a second while you work out that the church opposite is dedicated to St Sebastian, the patron saint of archers.

⑥⑦ Terrastje 🍷
45 Genthof
T 050 33 09 19
⊗ Wednesday & Thursday
🕐 10.30–23.30
🍸 46
🍴 Bar snacks of a regional variety

The Little Terrace is a little gem, just two hundred metres off the beaten track but better value and away from the hordes.

It gets its name from the wooden-decked area at the front of the bar. From here you have a good view of the canal over the road where cormorants can be seen fishing for eel and hanging their wings to dry on the wooden posts sticking up from the water.

Terrastje is a one-roomed cafe with friendly service. While it would be wrong to describe this as a restaurant, they cook traditional regional main courses and make waffles.

A new feature is a "beer of the month" which tends to promote one of the stronger beers.

The beer list runs to 46 choices and includes a few from the Regenboog brewery in Assebroek, on the outskirts of Bruges. However, unique in Bruges to our knowledge, they also have **Watou's Wit** (5%) from the Van Eecke brewery permanently on draught.

Van Eecke are famous for their Kapittel range of abbey-style beers and the hop-laden Poperings Hommelbier. Their cloudy wheat beer is said by many to be the best of its type in Belgium, with a wonderful lemon citrus and coriander flavour that is most refreshing, especially in summer.

68 **Tijl & Nele**
2 Jaacob Van Maerlantstraat (Damme)
T 050 35 71 92
F 050 37 22 94
E tijl.nele@pandora.be
http://users.pandora.be/tijlennele
⊗ Wednesday & Thursday (Oct–Mar); Friday
🕙 09.30–18.00
🍷 12
🥪 Sandwiches to take away

Damme's economc survival in the 21st century depends on preserving its image as the place that inspired much of Flemish literature. In particular, the work of Charles De Coster, who published in 1887 *Tijl Uilenspiegel*, the stories of a young joker of that name, his girlfriend Nele and their friend Lamme Goedzak.

Where English writers would have this crew embarrassing themselves and their families in public, the Tijl and Nele stories concentrate on the tricks they play to rid Flanders of the Spanish occupation. And of course, in the end, no longer the fool, Tijl becomes the hero.

The modern incarnation of Tijl en Nele in their home town is a pretty little shop that specialises in local food and drink, bicycle hire and sandwiches.

The selection of beers in the shop have been chosen for their local links, though in fact the Pater Van Damme Bruin is a rebadged version of the excellent **Potteloereke** (8%) from an exciting new microbrewery, Sint Canarus of Gottem in East Flanders. This darkish, red-brown strong ale can be drunk from special pottery mugs that can be bought in the shop too.

You would never guess that such a confident, mature, long-lasting caramel taste, touch of liquorice and warming finish could come from such a new brewery. It's a goodie.

Tuf Tuf 🍷
1 Ketsbruggestraat
📞 050 38 17 87
Tuesday
🍺 Su 11.00–22.00; Mo to 18.00;
We to 20.00; others to 10.00–23.00
🍷 19
🍴 Light snacks only

This wide-windowed, high set bar overlooks the station and transport hub of Bruges. It is a great waiting room from which to watch Bruges on the move and makes a good first and last café stop.

Tuf Tuf is also handy for the exhibitions set up on the square in front of the station at various times throughout the year, the most notable of which is the fantastic Snow and Ice Exhibition that runs from November to the New Year.

The café has a wide variety of small snacks to keep you going if your visit starts to string out. With each beer they serve a sizable bowl of very orange coloured crisps.

This is one of the few bars in the city that has the flagship beer from Antwerp's De Koninck brewery, called simply **De Koninck** (5%) on draught. It is a wonderfully rounded lightish pale ale that begs you to order another. If you are confident with your Dutch you can try ordering in the manner of an Antwerper, who would simply ask for a *bolleke*.

(Note: it's the name of the glass!)

Tuinbos

70 Tuinbos
678 Gistelsesteenweg
T 050 38 05 99
http://users.pandora.be/wtctuinbos
⊗ Tuesday
From 10.00
150
Sandwiches only

One of the great, undiscovered beer bars of Bruges. Out in the suburb of Sint Andries but well worth the trek. To get there catch bus no. 5, which runs every 20 minutes or so for much of the day from the railway station, t'Zand and Markt. Ask to get off at Hermitage.

Tuinbos succeeds because of the enthusiastic couple who run it generating a loyal local clientele. It is home to WTC Tuinbos, an enthusiastic bunch of cyclists drawn from all age groups. There is a summer terrace and plenty of parking. Inside is a pool table.

It has a fine beer list with strength in most areas. At Christmas they get in a variety of seasonal beers to put you in the spirit. All the Trappist breweries are represented here. Ask about any special beers, as not all are necessarily mentioned on the list in the café.

Although Regenboog brewery is on the outskirts of Bruges there are very few cafés in the city where you can drink their excellent beers. Tuinbos stocks most of them and from these we choose **'t Smisje Tripel** (9%) as one of the best. This hazy orange strong ale with background tastes of sweet fruits and spices really drinks its weight.

Uilenspiegel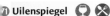
2 Langestraat
T 050 34 65 55
F 050 49 02 06
E info@uilenspiegelbvba.be
www.uilenspiegelbvba.be
Thursday (mid-Sep to mid-Mar)
We 08.00–14.00; others from 08.00
23
Full restaurant menu, including
Flemish and Greek menus

Another café named in reference to Charles De Coster's *Tijl Uilenspiegel*, the stories about the mythical "boy done good", who liberated Damme from the Spaniards.

The café is set at the junction of Langestraat, Predikherenrei and the canal. Its large outside drinking terrace is a great place to sit and watch the world and its boats go about their business. It can get busy in the summer.

The multi-lingual menu covers everything from small snacks through to the big Burgundian blow-outs, served indoors and out. They also do a neat line in Greek dishes.

The "house beer" is **Uilenspiegelbier** (8%), commissioned by the Damme Tourist Office from the Van Steenberge brewery near Ghent. It is ruddy brown and has sweet, malty, spicy flavours.

72 De Verloren Hoek
178 Carmersstraat
T 050 33 06 98
http://surf.to/verlorenhoek
⊗ Tuesday & Wednesday
Sa 10.30–14.00 & from 17.00;
others from 10.30
15
Substantial bar meals,
all home-made, include salad of
smoked duck breast and bacon hot-pot.

The Lost Corner is set just off the ring road opposite a huge windmill. This is one of two working windmills that survive from the many that used to surround the city walls, pumping water, grinding corn and being generally eco-friendly in a remarkably futuristic way.

Each of the survivors is still in working order and is used to grind flour. They are open to visitors every day in summer.

Despite the windmills, tourists rarely venture this far out of the centre of Bruges and this small, family-run tavern is busy mainly with local Brugeans, especially on a Sunday. One of the reasons for this is the excellent food, all home-prepared, on an interesting and ever-changing menu, in generous portions and at non-restaurant prices!

They also have private accommo-dation for rent.

The beer list is relatively limited but you can try **Dentergems** (5%), the wheat beer brewed by the Liefmans group at Dentergem. Although just as cloudy it is not as sweet or spicy as some wheat beers, though just as drinkable.

De Vlaamsche Pot

3–5 Helmstraat

T 050 34 00 86

F 050 34 00 86

E info@devlaamsschepot.be

www.devlaamschepot.be

Thursday

12.00–22.00

17

Full restaurant menu of traditional Flemish dishes

The Flemish Pot is a cute little restaurant found just off Noordzandstraat, between Markt and 't Zand. It is painted white with stepped gables and feels thoroughly Brugean both inside and out.

The theme extends to the food, which has an emphasis on grandmother-style Flemish dishes such as a creamy vegetable and chicken or fish *waterzooi*, *paling in 't groen* (eel in a chervil sauce), *stoofvlees* (slow-cooked beef stew) and rabbit cooked in a variety of ways.

A new addition to the beer menu is **Struise Witte** (5%), commissioned by De Struise Brouwers from the Deca brewery at Woesten, near the French border. The beers they commission help to publicise and subsidise their ostrich farm at Lo. They may yet open their own brewery one day.

This unfiltered, unpasteurised wheat beer has pretensions of greatness and leaves a flavourful and full-bodied aftertaste, unlike some better known brands.

Vlissinghe

74 Vlissinghe
2 Blekersstraat
T 050 34 37 37
F 050 34 37 37
E info@cafevlissinghe.be
www.cafevlissinghe.be
⊗ Monday & Tuesday
Su 10.00–19.00;
We&Th 11.00–24.00;
Fr&Sa from 11.00
♈ 23
Light snacks only

Vlissinghe is the oldest continuously licensed premise in Bruges, having functioned as some form of café, tavern or hostelry since 1515. Its interior impresses, with the Van Dyck armchair and old Brugean stove dominating the main room.

There is also well-kept polished copper and brassware, and pictures, porcelain and portraits on display throughout. Outside at the rear is a lovely garden with a pitch on which to play petanque (*boules*). Inside are board games for the less energetic.

Food is limited to pastas, *croques*, soups (in winter) and the ubiquitous pancakes with ice cream.

On the beer list you will find Van Eecke brewery's **Poperings Hommelbier** (7.5%), the hop beer of Poperinge. It is brewed at Watou, outside Poperinge, in the heart of Belgium's main hop growing area, one of the places where hops were first cultivated in the 13th century and have grown ever since.

This delightful beer delivers hops, not in the uncouth manner of a hop monster beer but with finesse. It can be enjoyed year-round but makes a surprisingly refreshing summer beer.

135 Carmersstraat

T 050 33 97 39

⊗ Saturday

🕐 10.00—22.00

🍷 22

🍴 Light snacks only

The Windmill is located out at the ring road end of Carmerstraat, opposite the Veloren Hoek (above). This gorgeous little café has a super view of one of the working windmills. When it is operating you can enjoy a great free show. The paddles get up quite a speed and you can really feel their power.

Against a background of exposed brickwork, its lovely interior is packed with cane chairs, old enamel drinks signs, birdcages, lamps, vehicle licence plates, coffee grinders, jugs, Singer sewing machines, witches, clowns, pot plants, hop festoons and of course, windmills.

The menu stretches to spaghetti, other pasta and omelettes and is also big on desserts, ice-creams and milkshakes.

One beer to try with any of the heavier desserts is the uncompromising **Kasteelbier Blond** (11%) from Van Honsebrouck. This sweet, golden beer drinks like a barley wine and leaves a warm afterburn like spiritous liquor.

76 't Zand 🍷 ✕ 🛏
21 't Zand
T 050 33 69 62
F 050 34 44 57
E info@cafetzand.be
www.hoteltzand.be
Open all week
🕐 From 09.00
🍷 23
🍴 Full restaurant menu including
spit-roast chicken and tapas

One of the newest additions to the
Bruges scene, a conversion of the old
Boudewijn Hotel and its bar into a
modern hotel-restaurant café business.

The huge café-restaurant now
consists of a single, smart, modern
room centred around a clear focal
point in the shape of a rotisserie.
You just have to order a *kip aan 't spit*,
half a roast chicken, to get why it is there.

There is a broader restaurant menu
also (12.00–15.00; 18.00–23.00) and a
tapas-style snack menu (11.00 onwards).
Plus pancakes.

Café 't Zand also offers one very unusual draught beer – **Echt Kriekenbier** (6.8%)
from the Verhaeghe brewery at Vichte
near Kortrijk. In recent years most
Belgian brewers have shied away from
expensive methods such as the slow
maturation of beers in oak, or steeping
whole fruit to make fruit beers. At
Verhaeghe they keep investing in new
oak tuns and insist on steeping whole
cherries in their aged brown beers.

This refusal to cut corners results
in a beer with a superb, full flavour.
The draught version is unpasteurised
and this dark red beer is possibly the
best fruity brown beer in the world.

Zandloper

AROUND BRUGES 77 IN 80 BEERS

77 De Zandloper
33 't Zand
T 050 34 13 46
Wednesday (Nov-Mar); Thursday
From 10.00
38
Full restaurant menu, with three-course set menus prominent

The Hour Glass is a large, one-roomed, bright, modern café-restaurant just off
't Zand, which features a bit more originality on its menu than the standard tourist fare on the main square.

Fish soup and proper home-made shrimp croquettes feature, together with rack of lamb, wok-fried creations and rabbit cooked in beer, along with the ubiquitous waffles, pancakes and ice cream.

In season they serve the deep, rich Corsendonk Christmas ale but year-round they also have a cherry beer from Boon brewery in 37.5cl corked bottles.

Frank Boon is almost unique among lambic brewers in prizing sumptuous fruit content in his lambics. His masterpiece is the rarely found Mariage Parfait Oude Kriek. **Kriek Boon** (5%) is their more widely available beer but still packs an immense fruity whole cherry taste with slight background lambic flavours.

Lambic virgins will find it easily palatable while serious beer enthusiasts will not find it as insulting as the syrupy versions from other brewers.

Zolder

78 De Zolder
53 Vlamingstraat
T 050 34 04 52
E dezolder_65@hotmail.com
http://drop.to/dezolder
⊗ Tuesday
Su from 18.00; others from 17.00
🍷 54
Bar snacks only

This atmospheric, medieval cellar bar is out along Vlamingstraat, a few minutes' walk from Markt. Located straight off the pavement, down a steep flight of stairs that has little headroom. It is easily missed so watch out for the Hommelbier A-board pointing the way.

The décor is well put together with an open fire, candlelit dark wood tables, brick archways and enamel brewery signs. The plaster and brick walls have various hangings, but the best by far are the old Flemish schoolroom maps with some pretty obvious howlers.

The food menu is limited but all is home-made and good value. The biggest it gets is *stoverij* (a beef stew) made with St Bernardus beer, a hearty chilli and spaghetti Bolognese.

Service is quick, courteous and well-informed and the beer menu is expertly chosen. It is strong on beers from Bavik and Sint Bernardus plus some interesting draught beers. Vichtenaar (from Verhaeghe), Abbaye des Rocs and Montagnarde (from Abbaye des Rocs) and Moinette (from Dupont) all stand out on the menu.

Our chosen beer for the Zolder is a unique fruit beer, **Oudbeitje** (6%). Hanssens do not brew lambics but carry on the traditions of steeping and blending the lambics of other breweries. This one is made from lambic that has aged on strawberries for six months. It is Belgium's only authentic strawberry lambic.

79 **In de Zwarte Kat** 🍷
  43 Balstraat
T 050 44 87 64
⊗ Monday
🕐 09.30–12.15 & 14.00–16.45
🍷 6
🍴 None

The Black Cat is an unusual café, set inside a museum (under 13 free; adults aged 27–64 €3,00; others €2,00).
It is designed deliberately as in times gone by, with an impressive old bar and a grandfather clock. There is a lovely old organ which will fire up and give you a loud tune if you oblige it with a 20 cent coin.

However, the real star is the Zwarte Kat itself, which stalks the museum. The present cat is the third in the dynasty and is fond of coffee drinkers, or more correctly their discarded milk pots. There is a collection box on the bar marked "Voor de kat" (for the cat). It makes you wonder what he spends it on.

The museum is housed in the low whitewashed almshouses of the old Shoemakers' Guild and aims to re-create life in old Bruges.

Separate buildings house a cooperage, a milliner's workshop, a spice store, a sweet shop and a selection of old pub signs. In summer you can play traditional games in the garden.

The museum's bar serves **Brugse Straffe Hendrik Blond** (6%), for many years THE beer of Bruges and originally made at the Halve Maan brewery on Walplein. Now brewed at Dentergem, it is still an excellent, tasty pale ale. Although not really a session beer, is easy to drink a number back to back.

Zwijntje

⑧⓪ 't Zwijntje 🍷 ✖
8 Hauwerstraat
T 050 34 43 48
F 050 34 43 48
✖ Sunday & Monday
🕐 Fr 11.30–23.30; Sa 09.30–23.30;
others 11.30–14.00 & 18.00–22.30
🍷 12
🍴 Full restaurant menu,
with several special pork dishes

The expression Little Pig, may sum up what you feel like after a weekend or longer in Bruges. In this case the name alludes to the fact that this café-restaurant does all things edible and drinkable to do with pigs.

You can dine on pork with raisins flambéed in calvedos, ribs, or *hammetje* (a large ham joint). For those who would prefer something with less grunt, there are also fish dishes and pasta.

The early opening hours on a Saturday are due to the huge market that runs from 't Zand along Hauwerstraat, directly in front of the café. This is usually for the regular weekly shopping but four times a year they hold a *rommelmarkt* or gigantic flea market, which expands to cover the surrounding streets from 't Zand right up to the station.

The house beer is called **Zwijntje** (8%) and is commissioned from Van Steenberge. Zwijntje beer is rebadged Augustijn with a piggy label and is tasty, blonde and hoppy.

Index of breweries and beers

Bruges is in the administrative centre for the province of West Flanders, roughly equivalent to an English county. About 40% of the beers featured in this book come from West Flanders, with the others coming from seven of the country's nine other provinces.

*signifies a Trappist abbey brewery where brewing is overseen by monks.

ANTWERP

Achel,* *from Achel on the Dutch border*
㊱ Achel Blond (8%)

Anker, *from the city of Mechelen*
㉖ Gouden Carolus Classic (8.5%)

De Koninck, *from the city of Antwerp*
(69) De Koninck (5%)

Moortgat, *from Breendonk, SW of Antwerp*
㊼ Duvel (8.5%)
(61) Maredsous 6 (6%)

Westmalle,* *from Westmalle, NE of Antwerp*
(58) Westmalle Dubbel (7%)
② Westmalle Tripel (9.5%)

EAST FLANDERS

Bosteels, *from Buggenhout, NW of Brussels*
㊴ Karmeliet Tripel (8%)
(56) Pauwel Kwak (8%)

Huyghe, *from Melle, SE of Ghent*
(62) Delirium Tremens (9%)
(54) Oxfam Blond (7.5%)

Malheur, *from Buggenhout, NW of Brussels*
㊸ Malheur 12 (12%)

Palm, *Steenhuffel, NW of Brussels*
㊳ Brugge Blond (6.5%)
(60) Brugge Tripel (8.2%)

Proef, *from Lochristi, NE of Ghent*
⑯ Reinaert Tripel (9%)

Roman, *from Oudenaarde, south of Ghent*
㊺ Ename Tripel (9%)

Sint Canarus, *from Gottem, SW of Ghent*
(68) Potteloereke (8%)

Slaghmuylder, *from Ninove, west of Brussels*
㉙ Witkap Stimulo (6%)

Van den Bossche, *from Sint-Lievens-Esse, SE of Ghent*
③ Pater Lieven Blond (6.5%)

Van Steenberge, *from Ertvelde, north of Ghent*
㉓ Augustijn (8%) *(aged draught)*
(80) *Augustijn (8%) (bottled)*
㉗ Basseveld Ezelsbier (9%)
(71) Uilenspiegelbier (8%)

FLEMISH BRABANT

Boon, *from Lembeek, south of Brussels*
(77) Boon Kriek (5%)
(57) Boon Oude Geuze (7%)

Cam (de), *from Gooik, SW of Brussels*
(53) De Cam Oude Kriek (6.5%)

Drie Fonteinen, *from Beersel, SW of Brussels*
㊶ Drie Fonteinen Oude Gueuze (6%)

Girardin, *from Sint-Ulriks-Kapelle, west of Brussels*
⑧ Girardin Oude Gueuze 1882 (5%)

Haacht, *from Bortmeerbeek, NE of Brussels*
⑩ Adler (6%)

Hanssens, *from Dworp, SW of Brussels*
(78) Hanssens Oudbeitje (6%)

Timmermans, *from Vlezenbeek, west of Brussels*
⑰ Bourgogne des Flandres (5.5%)

Index of breweries and beers

HAINAUT

Brunehaut, *from Rongy, south of Tournai*
㉛ Ramée Blonde (8%)
Chimay,* *from Scourmont, south of Charleroi*
㉔ Chimay Bleue (9%)

Dubuisson, *from Pipaix, east of Tournai*
④ Bush Ambrée (12%)

Dupont, *from Tourpes, east of Tournai*
⑭ Saison Dupont (6.5%)

Ellezelloise, *from Ellezelles, NE of Tournai*
㉒ Hercule (8.4%)

Ranke (de), *from Dottignies, south of Kortrijk*
㉕ XX Bitter (6.2%)

LUXEMBOURG

Achouffe, *from Achouffe, near Houffalize*
㊻ La Chouffe (8%)
㉚ McChouffe (8.5%)

Fantôme, *from Soy, near Erezée*
⑦ Fantôme (8%)

Orval,* *from Villers-devant-Orval, near Florenville*
㊷ Orval (6.2%)

Rulles, *from Rulles, west of Arlon*
⑮ Rulles Triple (8.3%)

NAMUR

Bocq (du), *from Purnode, south of Namur*
㉜ Corsendonk Agnus (7.5%)
㉘ Deugniet (7.3%)
(51) St Feuillien Blonde (7.5%)

Rochefort,* *from Rochefort, SE of Namur*
(52) Rochefort 8 (9.2%)
㊿ Rochefort 10 (11.3%)

WALLONIAN BRABANT

Lefèbvre, *from Quenast, SW of Brussels*
(66) Barbãr (8%)

WEST FLANDERS

Bavik, *from Bavikhove, NE of Kortrijk*
⑳ Bavik Ezel Wit (5.8%)
⑤ Pilaarbijter Blond (7.2%)

Deca, *from Woesten, near the French border*
① Pannepot (10%)
(73) Struise Wit (5%)
Dolle Brouwers, *from Esen, SW of Bruges*
㊵ Arabier (7%)
⑥ Oeral (6%)
⑬ Oerbier (7.5%)

Halve Maan, *from the city of Bruges*
㉟ Brugse Zot Blond (6%)
⑱ Brugse Zot Dubbel (7.5%)

Liefmans, *from Dentergem, NE of Kortrijk*
(79) Brugse Straffe Hendrik Blond (6%)
(63) Brugse Straffe Hendrik Bruin (8.5%)
(72) Dentergems (5%)
⑫ Liefmans Frambozenbier (5%)
(64) Liefmans Goudenband (8%)
⑨ Liefmans Kriekbier (6%)
㉞ Lucifer (8.5%)

Regenboog, *from Assebroek (Bruges)*
(70) 't Smisje Tripel (9%)

Rodenbach, *from the Roeselare, SW of Bruges*
㊲ Rodenbach (5%)
㊹ Rodenbach Grand Cru (6.5%)

Sint Bernardus, *from Watou, near the French border*
(59) Grottenbier (6.5%)
㊾ St Bernardus Abt 12 (10%)
㉝ St Bernardus Pater 6 (6.5%)
⑪ St Bernardus Prior 8
(55) St Bernardus Tripel (8%)

Strubbe, *from Ichtegem, SW of Bruges*
(65) Vlaskop (5.5%)

Van Eecke, *from Watou, near the French border*
(74) Poperings Hommelbier (7.5%)
(67) Watou's Wit (5%)

Van Honsebrouck, *from Ingelmunster, north of Kortrijk*
㉑ Brigand (9%)
(75) Kasteelbier Blond (11%)
㊽ Kasteelbier Bruin (12%)

Verhaeghe, *from Vichte, east of Kortrijk*
⑲ Duchesse de Bourgogne (6.2%)
(76) Echt Kriekenbier (6.8%)